Basketball
Handbook

by John Mills

 HANCOCK HOUSE PUBLISHERS

ISBN 0-88839-042-4 pa.

Copyright © 1980 Mills, John
Second Printing 1984

These books have been prepared for the Ministry of Education, Province of British Columbia, under the direction of the Secondary Physical Education Curriculum Revision Committee (1980)

James Appleby
Alex Carre
Madeline Gemmill
Gerry Gilmore
George Longstaff

John Lowther
Mike McKee
Norman Olenick
David Turkington

Handbook Consultant: F. Alex Carre, Ph.D.

Canadian Cataloguing in Publication Data

Mills, John.
    Basketball handbook and curriculum guide
(Physical education series)

    Bibliography: p.
    ISBN 0-88839-042-4 pa.
    1. Basketball - Training. I. Title.
II. Series: Physical Education Series (North Vancouver, B.C.)
GV885.35.M54   796.32'3'0712   C80-091144-X

All rights reserved. No part of this publication may be reproduced, stored in a retrieval system or transmitted in any form or by any means, electronic, mechanical, photocopying, recording or otherwise without the prior written permission of Hancock House Publishers.

Editor Margaret Campbell
Design Paul Willies & Donna White
Production Tom Morgan
Cover Photo Paul Bond
Typeset by Donna White *in Megaron type on an AM Varityper Comp/Edit*

Printed in Canada

Published by
HANCOCK HOUSE PUBLISHERS LTD.
#10 Orwell St. North Vancouver, B.C. V7J 3K1

Table of Contents

Acknowledgments 7
Court Diagram 7

Chapter One
Format and Purpose of the Handbook

    A. Introduction 8
    B. Purpose of the Handbook 8
    C. Handbook Format 8
    D. Objectives of the Program... 8
    E. Application to Classroom Teaching 8
    F. Description of the Levels Approach 8
    G. Explanation of Activity Sequence Chart 9
    H. Activity Sequence Chart 9
    I. Relationship of Basketball to Goals and Learning Outcomes 10

Chapter Two
Skill Development and Teaching Techniques

    A. Basic Skills 11
        1. Athletic Position 11
        2. Mobility 11
            a) Starting 11
            b) Running 11
            c) Change of direction 11
            d) Jump stop 12
            e) Stride stop 12
        3. Catching 12
    B. Individual Offensive Skills 13
        1. Passing 13
            a) Chest pass 13
            b) Bounce pass 14
            c) Two-hand overhead pass 14
            d) Baseball pass 14
        2. Dribbling 14
            a) Individual ball control 15
            b) Static dribbling 15
                i change of hands 15
            c) Motion dribbling 16
                i control dribble 16
                ii speed dribble 16
            d) Dodging 16
                i crossover dribble 17
                ii reverse dribble 17
            e) Dribbling against one defender 17
            f) Dribbling in a game situation 17
        3. Pivoting 18
        4. Shooting 18
            a) One-hand set shot 18

     i body and hand position 18
     ii arc 19
     iii backspin 19
     iv follow-through 20
  b) Free throw 20
  c) Jump shot 20
  d) Turn-around jump shot 20
  e) Hook shot 21
  f) Lay-up shot 21
  g) Variations of the lay-up 21
     i baseline lay-up 21
     ii underhand and overhand lay-up 21
     iii reverse lay-up 21
 5. Rebounding 21
  a) Defensive rebounding 22
     i obtaining position 22
     ii gaining possession 23
     iii outletting 23
  b) Offensive rebounding 23
  c) Shooting with an offensive rebound 24
 6. Faking 24
 7. Specialized Individual Techniques 24
  a) Jab and shoot 25
  b) Jab and go 25
  c) Jab, fake and go (rocker step) 25
  d) Jab and crossover 26
C. Individual Defensive Skills 26
 1. Stance 26
 2. Footwork 27
 3. Defending the Man with the Ball 27
  a) Defending the triple threat player 27
  b) Defending the dribbler 27
  c) Defending a dead dribble 28
 4. Defending the Man without the Ball 29
D Team Play 29
 1. Team Offensive Tactics - Man-to-Man 29
  a) Two-on-two 29
     i give and go 29
     ii the return hand off 30
     iii back door play 30
     iv screen and roll 30
  b) Three-on-three 31
     i screening away from the ball 31
     ii the post game 31
  c) Five-on-five - Principles 32
     i positional play 32
     ii shot selection 33
     iii ball movement 34
     iv conditioning and timing 34

- d) Building the half court offense 34
    - i two-on-two 34
    - ii three-on-three 35
    - iii four-on-four 35
    - iv half-court scrimmage (five-on-five) 35
- e) Special situations 36
    - i pass from out of bounds 36
    - ii jump ball 36
    - iii free throw attempts 37
2. Team Offensive Tactics - Zone 37
    - a) Principles 37
        - i rapid ball movement 37
        - ii team alignment 38
        - iii quick transition 38
        - iv penetration 38
3. Team Defensive Tactics - Man-to-Man 38
    - a) Principles 38
        - i floor position 38
        - ii communication 39
        - iii transition 39
        - iv ball side, help side 39
    - b) Two-on-two 40
        - i defending the give and go 40
        - ii defending the screen and roll 40
    - c) Three-on-three 41
        - i defending the screen away 41
    - d) Guarding the post 41
4. Team Defensive Tactics - Zone 42
    - a) Principles 42
    - b) Zone alignments 42
- E. Rules 43
- F. Officiating 44

Chapter Three
Drills
- A. Basic Skills 46
    1. Free Movement, Change of Direction 46
    2. Partner Shadow 46
- B. Passing Drills 46
    1. Box Drill 46
    2. Fake, Fake, Fake! 46
    3. Pig in the Middle 46
    4. Two-player Technique Perfection Drill 47
    5. Turnaround 47
    6. Keep Away 47
    7. Pass and Pivot Relay 47
    8. Circle Passing Drill 47
    9. Bull in the Ring 47

        10. Shell Drill 47
        11. Baseball Pass Drill 48
    C. Dribbling and Footwork Drills 48
        1. Check Control Dribbling Drill 48
        2. Dribble Tag 48
        3. Speed and Control Dribble Relays 48
        4. Stop and Go Drill 48
        5. Line Dribble 48
        6. Zigzag Drill 48
    D. Dribbling and Ball Handling Drills 48
        1. Dribble Catch 48
        2. Hand Sensitiser Drill 49
        3. Dribbling on the Knees 49
        4. Two-hand Dribbling 49
        5. Straight Line Dribble 49
        6. Figure Eight Drill 49
        7. Around the Body and Legs 49
        8. Reverse dribble Tag 49
    E. Shooting Drills 49
        1. Around the Gym Relay 49
        2. Two Against the Rebounder 49
        3. Rebound Block-Out Drill 49
        4. Basket Golf 49
        5. Hot Shot Drill 50
        6. Twenty-One Shooting Drill 50
    F. Modified Games 50
        1. Platoon Basketball 50
        2. Guard Ball 50
        3. Bucket Ball 50
        4. One-on-One Drill 51
        5. Two-on-Two Drill 51
        6. Three-on-Three Drill 51

Chapter Four
Sample Lesson Plans
    Lesson One: Rules and Principles of the Game 52
    Lesson Two: Passing and Receiving 52
    Lesson Three: Footwork and Ball Handling 53
    Lesson Four: Shooting 54
    Lesson Five: One-on-One Basketball (Offense and Defense) 54
    Lesson Six: Two-on-Two Basketball (Multi-Level Lesson) 55
    Lesson Seven: Three-on-Three Basketball 55
    Lesson Eight: Team Play - Offense 56
    Lesson Nine: Team Play - Defense 56
    Lesson Ten: The Tournament 57

Chapter Five
Evaluation
   A. Program Evaluation 58
   B. Player Evaluation 58

Appendix I
Reference Material 62

Appendix II
Dr. James Naismith's Original Basketball Rules 63

Appendix III
Glossary 64

Acknowledgments

  To my wife Sheila who has supported all my efforts on behalf of Basketball.
  To the coaches, administrators, and officials whose dedication to Basketball is immeasurable.
  To the Players.

FULL SIZE REGULATION COURT

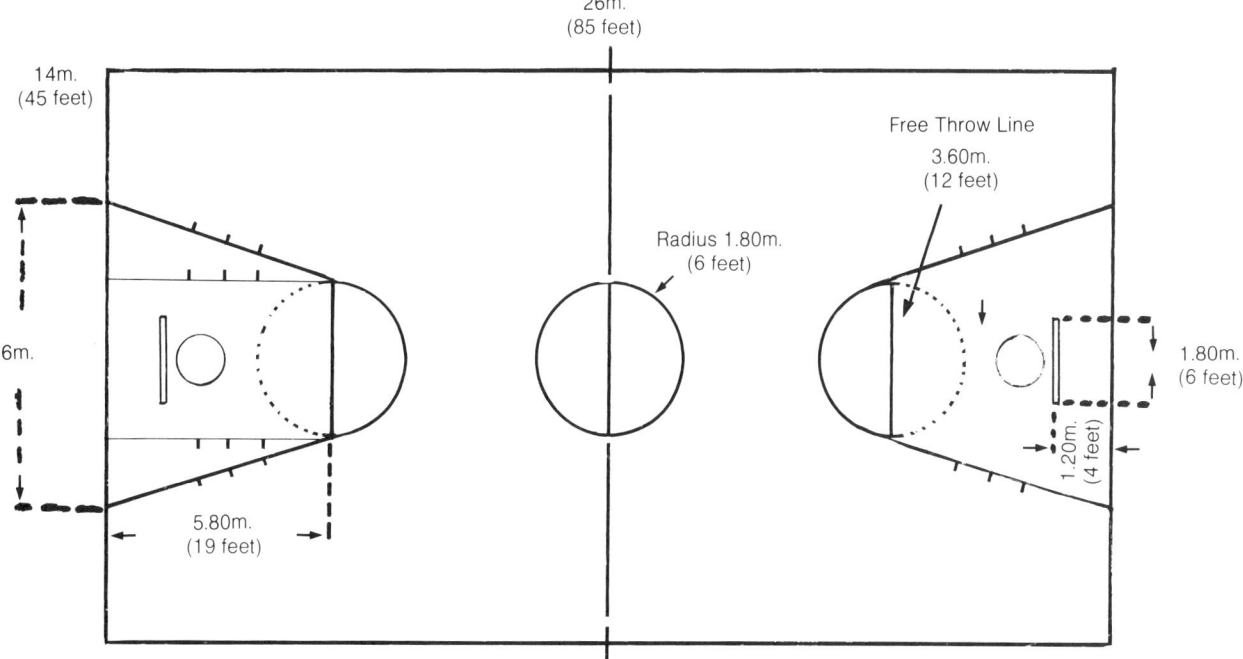

Note: The size of the restricted area or key may vary from place to place. The international key as outlined in the F.I.B.A. rules is trapezoidal in shape. The narrow or N.C.A.A. key is rectangular. Both keys are shown in the diagram and should appear on all basketball courts. The diagrams used later on in this book employ the narrow key.

Chapter One
Format and Purpose of the Handbook

A. Introduction: Why Play Basketball?

Everyone can benefit from exposure to a team sport. The concept of subordinating individual goals to those of a larger group are essential to the spirit of cooperation and community action on which contemporary society is founded. Basketball offers everyone the opportunity to take part, either recreationally or competitively, in an inexpensive, healthy sport that can be played for as long as a person is able to run. In fact, with minor rule adjustments to eliminate the fast break, adults are remaining active into their retirement years in the sport which they enjoyed so much as youngsters.

However, unlike many individual sports, adults seldom take up basketball if they have not been exposed to it during their school days. For this reason, it is important that all students receive instruction on the game's fundamentals, so that in later years they will feel comfortable as players and knowledgeable as spectators.

B. Purpose of the Handbook

This handbook is a specific extension of the Secondary Physical Education Curriculum and Resource Guide (1980). The information included in the handbook is designed to provide the instructor with a comprehensive source of information for the teaching of Basketball.

C. Handbook Format

The handbook describes in detail the skills required for playing Basketball and the recommended techniques for teaching them, suggests drills which can be used to practice these skills, offers sample lesson plans for the use of the instructor, and discusses methods of evaluation. The guidelines presented in this handbook are suggestions only and may be adapted as the instructor becomes more familiar with Basketball.

D. Objectives of the Program

The Basketball program has three major objectives:

1. Psychomotor Objectives
   a) Players should be able to perform skills in a game situation as a contributing team member.
   b) Players will experience increased fitness as a result of drill execution, practice and games.

2. Cognitive Objectives
   a) Players will understand the rules of the game and the principles upon which they are based.
   b) Players will understand and appreciate the function of the various officials (floor and table) as they pertain to the proper administration of a game.
   c) Players will be able to comment intelligently on and critically analyze plays they have observed.

3. Affective Objectives
   a) Players will appreciate the role basketball can play in their individual plan for lifetime fitness.
   b) Players will experience and appreciate the value of team work, and the satisfaction therein.
   c) Players will realize the importance of sportsmanship.

E. Application to Classroom Teaching

Basketball can be taught in such a fashion that in a class with a wide variance of skill levels and background, all can participate and achieve success. In order to do this, a program must be developed to suit individual differences, without overemphasizing (by segregation or restriction) the differences between individual players.

Basketball is a team game, a game in which team mates must appreciate the assets and liabilities of one another. A class can be organized along similar lines, with space for the less gifted and the beginners, as well as the highly skilled and experienced.

F. Description of Levels Approach

The teaching of Basketball should begin with simple activities and progress to the more complex. However, in a comprehensive Physical Education curriculum, emphasis should be placed on the provision of a sound framework for individual development, and progress must depend on the capabilities of the individual player rather than being determined by a grade level. One way of doing this is to use a sequentially developed program of physical activities that integrates affective, cognitive and psychomotor areas. This focus is called a "levels" approach.

Basketball uses a four-level system as follows:

Level I - Beginner
Level II - Novice
Level III - Intermediate
Level IV - Advanced

Each level introduces and develops some of the essential skills. The successive levels reinforce the existing skills and introduce new material in sequence. This process allows the basic skills and practical application to become thoroughly developed in a variety of situations.

In order to implement such a program, the instructor must:

a) Determine the starting point of each player. Is a player beginning at Level I, Level II, etc.?
b) What background does the player have? Has the player taken basketball before? At what level?

G. Explanation of Activity Sequence Chart

The Activity Sequence Chart outlines a progressive pattern of psychomotor and cognitive skills that are required for Basketball. The chart serves as a guide in planning sessions and indicates the level at which each skill should most likely be introduced. As learning continues, a skill is reinforced and built upon. For example, dribbling is introduced as a Level I skill and subsequent activities will reinforce this skill at other levels.

The instructor may refer to Chapter Two and Chapter Four for further assistance and more detailed information.

H. Activity Sequence Chart

SKILLS	I	II	III	IV
A. Basic Skills				
1. Athletic Position				
2. Mobility				
a) Starting		●		
b) Running		●		
c) Change of direction		●		
d) Jump stop		●		
e) Stride stop			●	
3. Catching		●		
B. Individual Offensive Skills				
1. Passing				
a) Chest pass		●		
b) Bounce pass		●		
c) Two-hand overhead pass		●		

SKILLS	I	II	III	IV
d) Baseball pass			●	
2. Dribbling				
a) Individual ball control	●			
b) Static dribbling	●			
i change of hands	●			
c) Motion dribbling				
i control dribble	●			
ii speed dribble	●			
d) Dodging			●	
i crossover dribble			●	
ii reverse dribble			●	
e) Dribbling against one defender		●		
f) Dribbling in a game situation			●	
3. Pivoting		●		
4. Shooting				
a) One-hand set shot	●			
i body and hand position				
ii arc				
iii backspin				
iv follow-through				
b) Free throw	●			
c) Jump shot			●	
d) Turn-around jump shot				●
e) Hook shot			●	
f) Lay-up shot	●			
g) Variations of the lay-up				
i baseline lay-up			●	
ii underhand and overhand lay-up			●	
iii reverse lay-up			●	
5. Rebounding				
a) Defensive rebounding				
i obtaining position		●		
ii gaining possession		●		
iii outletting		●		
b) Offensive rebounding		●		
c) Shooting with an offensive rebound		●		
6. Faking			●	
7. Specialized Individual Techniques				
a) Jab and shoot	●			
b) Jab and go			●	
c) Jab, fake and go (rocker step)				●

SKILLS	LEVELS			
	I	II	III	IV
d) Jab and crossover		•		
C. Individual Defensive Skills				
1. Stance	•			
2. Footwork	•			
3. Defending the man with the ball				
a) Defending the triple threat player	•			
b) Defending the dribbler	•			
c) Defending a dead dribble	•			
4. Defending the man without the ball		•		
D. Team Play				
1. Team Offensive Tactics - Man-to-Man				
a) Two-on-two	•			
i give and go		•		
ii the return hand off		•		
iii back door play			•	
iv screen and roll				•
b) Three-on-three	•			
i screening away from the ball			•	
ii the post game			•	
c) Five-on-five - Principles	•			
i positional play				
ii shot selection				
iii ball movement				
iv conditioning and timing				
d) Building the half court offense				
i two-on-two	•			
ii three-on-three	•			
iii four-on-four	•			
iv half-court scrimmage (five-on-five)	•			
e) Special situations				
i pass from out of bounds	•			
ii jump ball	•			
iii free throw attempts	•			
2. Team Offensive Tactics - Zone				
a) Principles				•
3. Team Defensive Tactics - Man-to-Man				
a) Principles				
i floor position	•			
ii communication	•			

SKILLS	LEVELS			
	I	II	III	IV
iii transition		•		
iv ball side, help side		•		
b) Two-on-two				
i defending the give and go		•		
ii defending the screen and roll				•
c) Three-on-three				
i defending the screen away		•		
d) Guarding the post		•		
4. Team Defensive Tactics - Zone				
a) Zone principles				•
b) Zone alignments				•
E. Rules	•			
F. Officiating			•	

I. Relationship of Basketball to Goals and Learning Outcomes

A series of Goals and Learning Outcomes for physical education were developed for the Secondary Physical Education Curriculum and Resource Guide (1980). The relationship of basketball to this Curriculum Guide is indicated below:

Active participation in a sound Basketball program should accomplish the following goals:

1. Players should demonstrate increased fitness.
2. Players should demonstrate improved skills and be able to participate as contributing members of a team.
3. Players should demonstrate an understanding of the rules and principles of the game, and be able to analyze each play.
4. Players should demonstrate a positive attitude towards Basketball as a lifetime activity and show an appreciation of the value of teamwork and sportsmanship.

Chapter Two
Skill Development and Teaching Techniques

A. Basic Skills

SKILL	DESCRIPTION	TEACHING TECHNIQUES AND OBSERVATION POINTS

1. Athletic Position

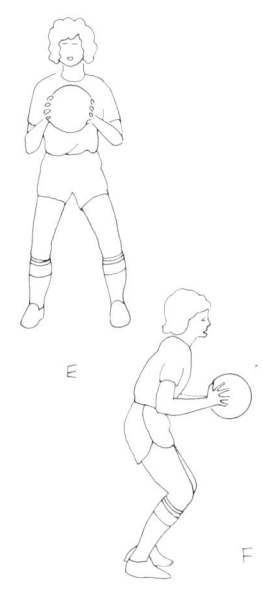

Players will find themselves in this position for a good portion of the game. It is not a stance characteristic only of Basketball. Most sports, where quick reactions are necessary, require a player to adopt such a stance. Arm and hand positions vary but the body position remains roughly the same for a baseball shortstop, a tennis player awaiting a serve, or a football linebacker. In fact the Basketball player will adjust this stance to suit different situations: defence against the dribbler, offense with the ball, and offense without the ball.

1. Feet should be shoulder width apart, or slightly wider. They may be staggered slightly.
2. Back straight, head erect, knees flexed.
3. The full soles of both feet should be on the floor but weight may be slightly forward on the balls of the feet.
4. Hand and arm position appropriate for offense or defense. (See Individual Defensive Skills for more information on hand and arm position).

2. Mobility

  a) Starting

Players should push off with the back foot, and step in the desired direction.

1. Movement on the court should be quick, controlled, and direct.
2. Players should move in straight lines whenever possible.
3. The initial body lean is exaggerated to build momentum.
4. Players should achieve a speed at which they are in complete control of their bodies rather than maximum speed.

  b) Running

Players are to move quickly and under control.

1. The rules expect players to be in complete control to the extent that they may be penalized for initiating contact with an opponent.
2. Players are balanced and erect.

  c) Change of direction

To change direction, a player plants the outside foot and steps in the intended

1. Many experts believe that the better the level of play, the more the players move in straight lines. Therefore any change of direction should be at a sharp angle rather than a rounded corner.

SKILL	DESCRIPTION	TEACHING TECHNIQUES AND OBSERVATION POINTS
	direction with the inside foot. For example, a player who wishes to cut to the right should plant the left foot and step to the right with the right foot.	
d) Jump stop 	a) A player stops by jumping off one foot and landing on both feet simultaneously. b) Feet land parallel. c) Player's knees are flexed to absorb forward momentum.	1. After take off, players lean backwards. 2. The faster the speed, the more exaggerated the backward lean. 3. The advantage of stopping in this fashion is that either foot may be used as the pivot for a subsequent fake or drive to the basket. Young players learn this skill quite quickly.
e) Stride stop	This is a quicker, more deceptive movement. It requires a player to absorb most of the shock of stopping with one leg. The other leg stops parallel to, or slightly ahead of the first foot. When we walk, we all use the stride stop. We plant one foot and bring the other foot beside it.	1. Most stride stops end with the placement of the second foot so that the body is square to the basket. This may necessitate a slight pivot. 2. As in the jump stop, the backward body lean is accentuated. 3. The knees should be flexed and ready to absorb the shock of stopping.
3. Catching	A receiver has as much to do with the success of a pass as the passer does. Unfortunately, instructors and coaches often overlook the techniques and learning potential in this fundamental aspect of the game. Too often players are labelled as having "good" or "bad" hands, and left on their own.	1. Players must make every effort to catch the ball with two hands. Just because there are more passes thrown in a basketball game than there are in a football game does not make the ball any less valuable. A football player would never catch with one hand when he could use two. Nor should a basketball player. 2. A receiver must give the passer a target by holding hands out where the receiver wants the ball thrown. This target should be away from the defense. 3. Always catch with one palm facing the ball to block its flight. This will eliminate the instance of a ball flying through the player's hands. 4. Players must always expect the pass. It is a player's responsibility to know where the ball is at all times, and therefore to expect to be thrown a pass. 5. Players must move toward the ball as it is passed. This will prevent an opponent from sneaking in to deflect or intercept the ball. 6. Acknowledge the passer after the play is over. A clever pass should be appreciated, and the passer complimented. 7. When possible, players should catch the ball facing the hoop, so they will be in position to see a team mate who may be in better scoring position. Players must work hard to make themselves available for a pass. They must use "V" or "angle" cuts. They should take a couple of hard steps in one direction, forcing their check to adjust position, then cut sharply in another direction.

SKILL	DESCRIPTION	TEACHING TECHNIQUES AND OBSERVATION POINTS
		8. In games and scrimmages, players should work to receive the pass in shooting position.

B. Individual Offensive Skills

SKILL	DESCRIPTION	TEACHING TECHNIQUES AND OBSERVATION POINTS
	Although Basketball is a team game, there are many instances where it boils down to one-on-one.	1. The offensive player has an opportunity to try to beat the defender for a score. In so doing, many skills will have to be integrated into a solo attack on the goal. Players should constantly be reminded, however, that in the game there will be eight other players on the court, in addition to themselves and their defender, and that they should not become preoccupied with individual moves to the exclusion of what is happening elsewhere. 2. The offensive player must take what the defense offers. Moves cannot be predetermined. Many players decide far in advance what they are going to do when they get the ball. This is a mistake. The defense must be read, and reacted to. For example, if an opponent is over-playing to the right, the offensive player should give a quick right fake, then drive to the left. If the defender's hands are down, the offense should shoot. 3. Players must be balanced and under control so that they can react instantly.
1. Passing	Passing is the quickest way to advance the ball against the defense, and is probably the fundamental component of successful team play. A team that can locate the open player and deliver the ball time after time is almost assured of success.	1. The simplest form of ball handling is holding the ball. 2. The ball should be held with both hands so that it is above the waist and close to the torso. 3. Movements with the ball should be quick. 4. Accuracy, of course, is essential in passing and should not be sacrificed.
a) Chest pass	This most elemental pass gets its name from the area in which the pass is generated. A pushing motion begins the pass, with the ball held in two hands close to the passer's chest. The pass concludes with full arm extension and the four fingers of both hands pointing at the receiver. The wrists will have rotated so that the palms will be facing slightly outward. Thumbs should point to the floor.	1. Younger and less physically mature players may need to step toward the receiver in order to generate sufficient force to pass the ball crisply. Stronger players should attempt to pass without moving either foot. If a player needs to step, the defense can "read" the pass as soon as the foot is lifted. This can be a disadvantage for the passer. 2. The chest pass should be thrown only when there is no threat of interception or deflection. The pass travels from chest level of the passer to chest level of the receiver. Use one of the two following passes when there is a defender between passer and receiver. 3. The ball must have reverse rotation or backspin. This eliminates the often erratic trajectory that a ball can take if it is not spinning.

SKILL	DESCRIPTION	TEACHING TECHNIQUES AND OBSERVATION POINTS
b) Bounce pass	The pass begins like a chest pass, but the ball bounces once between passer and receiver. This is a very useful, penetrating pass when the ball must be passed through or by a defender.	1. The ball should bounce closer to the receiver than to the passer. A good bounce pass generally covers three-quarters of the distance between passer and receiver before it bounces. 2. Again, this pass must be thrown with a backspin.
c) Two-hand overhead pass	Whenever a player is being pressured, this is an effective pass. It requires less power than the chest pass, and it gets the ball above the extended arms of the defender. The windup is minimal, and faking is easy. The overhead position is also close to the shooting position, making it possible for a player to fake the overhead pass and very quickly shoot the jump shot.	1. Instructors should encourage short, sharp fakes in this position. 2. Players must follow through on their passes. 3. The two-hand overhead pass should be crisply thrown.
d) Baseball pass 	The techniques for throwing the three previous passes are quite simple. In fact, most players can throw these passes correctly after only a few minutes practice. Some correction may be needed in the area of backspin. However, the baseball pass is more difficult, perhaps because it normally covers more distance than the other three passes, and therefore has a tendency to be less accurate. However, it is an important pass and certainly should not be overlooked.	1. As the name implies, the ball is thrown as one would throw a baseball. The ball is taken back with one hand and released overhead as the ball travels over the ear. However, as in baseball, some players tend to throw this pass with an incorrect wrist turn, thereby imparting not backspin but sidespin to the ball. Again, as in baseball, over a long distance this can result in inaccuracy. The ball can tail off the line on which it was thrown, like a curve ball. 2. A player who is throwing a ball with the right hand, should step forward with the left foot, being sure to follow through with the right hand. 3. The right forefinger should end up pointing to the ground. Some players finish the baseball pass with their forefinger pointing sideways, or even up, which imparts considerable sidespin to the ball. The forefinger should be pointing straight down, thereby ensuring that the pass is traveling with just backspin and not sidespin. 3. Players can and should become competent baseball passers with their weak hands, also. It takes only a little practice each day to build up the necessary strength and coordination.
2. Dribbling	Since a player who wishes to retain possession of the ball may not advance the ball by walking with it, the rules permit two options (dribbling and pivoting)- by which the ball may be protected from opponents,	

SKILL	DESCRIPTION	TEACHING TECHNIQUES AND OBSERVATION POINTS
	or the view of the court and team mates improved.	
a) Individual ball control	Dribbling is a skill by which a player may advance the ball while still retaining possession.	1. The skill consists of bouncing the ball with one hand while either running, walking, or standing. The dribble may be used judiciously and purposefully (see Building the half court offense, page 34.) Excessive dribbling slows the pace of the game. In addition, a player who has stopped dribbling but retained possession is less dangerous to the defense because that player's options have been limited to passing or shooting. 2. The rules of the game govern dribbling in two other major areas. To begin a dribble a player must keep the pivot foot still until the dribble has begun, that is until the ball begins its downward motion to the floor. Also, a player may not allow the ball to come to rest in the hands during the dribble. Should this occur, the player would have committed a violation and the ball will be given to the opposing team. 3. Some time should be spent demonstrating the rules as they pertain to dribbling and ball control. 4. Although a player will always experience some sort of defensive pressure in a game, it is often important that such external factors be removed when a player first tries to master the mechanics of dribbling. In most cases this does not take a prolonged period of time. Usually, after one day, a beginner can learn to distinguish between correct pushing action and the incorrect slap at the ball. 5. A variety of ball control drills can be done while stationary and these help to develop familiarity with the basketball. Perhaps they could even be employed daily as a very brief warm-up. 6. Instructors must be wary of spending great lengths of time teaching drills that may be entertaining and often very difficult, but have no practical application to the game of Basketball. Please refer to the introduction to the chapter on drills.
b) Static dribbling	Players must first learn to dribble the ball in place. It is easiest to start with all players on their knees sitting back on their heels. Once the static dribble is mastered from this position, the players should then stand. Players should be encouraged to learn to dribble with either hand and to avoid watching the ball.	1. Proper hand position: while on both knees and with the ball on the floor, beside the right knee, the player's right hand should be placed on top of the ball. Fingers should be spread comfortably, but not stretched. The heel of the hand should not be in contact with the ball. This is the basic hand position for dribbling. 2. The ball is pushed firmly downward with the combined forces of elbow and wrist. Finger position remains more or less the same, but the flexing of both the wrist and the elbow results in the fingers pointing to the floor after each dribble. This downward push should be firm, with the ball returning quickly. 3. The hand, wrist, and elbow cushion the ball as it returns, and then push it back down.
i Change of hands	Since a player must try to protect the ball from the	1. Again, it is probably easiest to teach this if the players have both knees on the floor.

SKILL	DESCRIPTION	TEACHING TECHNIQUES AND OBSERVATION POINTS
	defense, the player's body should be kept between the ball and the defender. To do this, a player must be able to dribble with both hands and to change the dribble from hand to hand at a moment's notice.	2. Players change hands by pushing the ball diagonally. As the ball comes up, they contact it on the side with the palm. 3. Slapping at the ball, particularly with the weak hand, should not be permitted.
c) Motion dribbling	This involves dribbling the ball while walking or running in a straight line. There are two types of dribble that can be used, the speed dribble and the control dribble.	1. Players must learn to control the ball before trying to increase speed. 2. Don't hesitate to have the players walk the ball if they can't run and dribble under complete control. 3. Once the drive to the hoop is begun, it should be in a straight rather than a curving line. Players should cut as close to their opponents as they can without contacting them.
i Control dribble	The control dribble is used in congested areas where possession is harder to maintain. The ball is allowed to rise slightly above knee level and is kept quite close to the dribbler's body. The essential difference is that the ball is out of the dribbler's control for only a brief instant when the height of the bounce is reduced. This gives the dribbler the extra control needed in close quarters.	
ii Speed dribble	The speed dribble is for peak speed movement with little close defensive pressure. The ball is allowed to rise to waist level and is pushed out in front of the body with each dribble.	
d) Dodging	The footwork for dodging or change of direction dribbling is the same as the footwork discussed under Running. This can be very reassuring to a beginning player who may be baffled by the ball handling, let alone the footwork.	

SKILL	DESCRIPTION	TEACHING TECHNIQUES AND OBSERVATION POINTS
i Crossover dribble	This is simply a simultaneous change of hands and direction executed in front of the dribbler.	1. The player plants the right foot if dribbling right-handed. 2. The player steps in the desired direction with the left foot. 3. The player then pushes the ball with the right hand so it bounces beyond the left foot. 4. As the ball travels across the body, the right foot steps and follows the ball so that as the ball comes up off the bounce the right leg is between it and the defender as protection. 5. The dribbler continues dribbling with the left hand. 6. The crossover dribble should be low and should cover as much ground as possible.
ii Reverse dribble	Here the player turns the back on the defense while changing hands and direction. It is especially useful when the dribbler is closely guarded.	1. A player who is dribbling in a right direction with the right hand plants the left foot and executes a reverse pivot. 2. A good teaching strategy is to have the players practice the footwork without the ball by either walking or running. 3. The left foot should be planted as the ball is coming up to the right hand. The right hand should be cupped slightly to pull the ball as it comes up. 4. Execute the pivot (see page 18) and swing the right foot so that it points in the desired direction. Pull the ball with the right hand and bounce it so that it lands directly in front of the dribbler. As the ball moves across, the left leg follows it and the dribble is picked up with the left hand. 5. The dribble that actually changes the ball's direction is made with the right hand. The left hand just picks up the dribble after both the pivot and the ball direction change have been made.
e) Dribbling against one defender	Most players can pick up the very basic elements of dribbling: hand position, arm position, and the proper footwork - in 10 to 15 minutes.	1. Once the players have learned and understood the technique, face each player with a defender so that all of their learning about ball handling from that time on is against some sort of defensive pressure. Make sure this defensive pressure does not intimidate the beginner, but it is crucial that there be the obligation for the dribbler to protect the ball and that if this is not done adequately, the ball may be stolen by the defender. Initially, the player should be required only to dribble the ball between two points, say, from the baseline to half-court, against some defensive pressure. It is not necessary to require the dribbler to try to score. 2. The players may use all the tools taught previously: the change of direction, the speed dribble, the control dribble. 3. Instructors should be very careful, in the initial stages of this dribbling against one defender, that the dribbler does not revert to slapping at the ball, or to previous errors in dribbling. Try to see whether each dribbler is performing the technique of dribbling properly. 4. Encourage players to turn their backs as little as possible. 5. The object is to move the ball from place to place as quickly as possible, and players should all understand that.
f) Dribbling in a game situation	Here the player must deal with more variables, notably the option of dribbling or passing to an	1. The basic teaching points discussed in the other sub-topics still apply: head up, back straight, knees flexed, etc. 2. Check out the defense. Upon reception of the ball, players should pivot and face up court, so they can see their team

SKILL	DESCRIPTION	TEACHING TECHNIQUES AND OBSERVATION POINTS
	open team mate. The player must use the dribble prudently to advance the ball up court and generate the score. Although this skill is valuable for any player, most teams are considered fortunate if they have one or two players who can consistently thwart full-court defensive pressure with the dribble or the pass.	mates and the defense deployed against them. Once all nine players are in front, an offensive player should begin to advance the ball against the defender, using the skills previously learned, but watching for one of the four team mates to shake free at any moment to receive a pass. 3. Players should anticipate a double team. 4. Once a player has begun to dribble, the move should not stop unless the player has decided what to do with the ball; that is, either pass the ball or shoot it. A player should not stop a dribble unnecessarily. 5. A player should cross mid-court near the center circle if possible. Doing so near the sideline invites a double team.
3. Pivoting	To pivot means to move one foot in any direction while the other remains in contact with the ground. The foot that remains stationary is called the pivot foot. The pivoting player's body should stay between the ball and the defender. In addition to protecting the ball, the pivot allows the player to turn to face the basket without dribbling.	1. Players should practice using either foot as the pivot foot, bearing in mind that in a game they may only use one pivot foot per possession. 2. Players must keep two hands on the ball at all times. The ball should be moving during the pivot so the defense cannot steal it. 3. The pivot foot is anchored until the ball is either passed, dribbled, or shot. Dragging the pivot foot is a rule violation. 4. The pivot may be executed either clockwise or counter-clockwise. Depending on which foot is the pivot foot, these motions can be termed front or reverse pivots. A clockwise pivot with the left foot anchored is a reverse pivot. 5. Pivoting is an important aspect of rebounding and will be discussed in that context in a later section.
4. Shooting	The single most important skill in basketball is shooting. There are several successful techniques, but all good shooters have a number of things in common. A good shooter's shot will have a reasonably high arc, it will have backspin, and the good shooter will follow through.	
a) One-hand set shot	i Body and hand position	1. Like most fundamentals, shooting begins from the basic athletic position. Knees should be flexed, the back straight, and the head erect. 2. The player holds the ball anywhere between waist and eye level, the dominant hand grasping the ball across the seams in the middle of the ball, the weak hand to the side of the ball. If the shooter is holding the ball at waist level, the dominant hand would be on top of the ball. If the shooter is holding the ball at eye level, the dominant hand would be beneath the ball. 3. Generally speaking, weaker players and, in most cases, younger players, will begin with the ball fairly low, around waist level, and will bring the ball up through the center of the body to generate some momentum and then release

SKILL	DESCRIPTION	TEACHING TECHNIQUES AND OBSERVATION POINTS

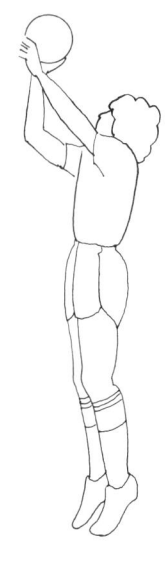

the ball in front of the face, or slightly above the face.
4. Players should be discouraged from shooting the ball with two hands, that is, from imparting force on the ball with two hands. It is important that the weak hand simply acts as a guide. Its function is much like that of the tee in golf; it is simply there to position the ball so that the strong hand can do the work.
5. In order to teach players proper hand position on the ball, it is worthwhile having the player stand, holding the ball upright with one hand. The elbow should be bent 90°, and the ball should be resting on the hand directly above the elbow. This will give the player the proper hand position. The ball should be resting on the fingers and the outside of the palm. The very center of the palm should be the only part of the hand not touching the ball.
6. When players are in the basic athletic position they may, if they feel comfortable doing so, stand with their feet slightly staggered. A right-handed shooter may prefer to shoot with the right foot forward; a left-handed shooter, with the left foot slightly forward. As players become more proficient, they should be able to shoot with their feet in virtually any position, provided they are balanced. This in fact becomes a distinct advantage as will be discussed in one-on-one offense.

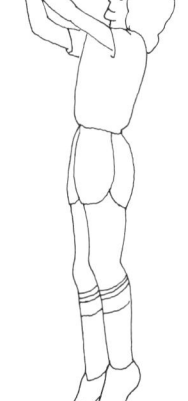

ii Arc

1. The trajectory of the ball's flight must be high enough for the ball to clear the front rim and drop into the hoop before hitting the back rim. It is easy for an adult to visualize how a flat shot will carry the front rim, yet likely hit the back rim and bounce out. Young players need a selling job to convince them that their shots should have an arc.
2. Have the players stand in a large circle that surrounds the center circle. The diameter of this circle of players is the distance from sideline to sideline. All are equidistant from the center circle. Ask the players to take a good look at the center circle while they are standing, and see how large the circle appears.
3. Then have them lie down with their chins on the floor and look at the same circle. In that position it doesn't appear to be a circle at all. In fact, it looks more like a very narrow oval.
4. This demonstration should illustrate to them that a shot with high arc has much more of the basket to go through than a shot with low arc.

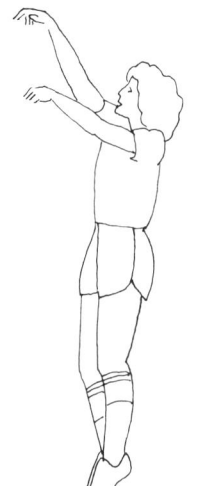

iii Backspin

1. If a shot has no backspin it could flutter the same as a pass with no backspin. More importantly, however, backspin tends to stop the forward motion of the ball. Backspin causes the ball to "die" when it hits the hoop. Unsuccessful shots with lots of backspin tend to rebound closer to the hoop than those shots without backspin. A good percentage of shots that don't go in cleanly will roll around the hoop and drop in if they left the shooter's hand with lots of backspin.
2. With the group of players viewing from the side, throw an underhand pass with no backspin. Watch it bounce, and

SKILL	DESCRIPTION	TEACHING TECHNIQUES AND OBSERVATION POINTS
		point out that the ball hits and keeps bouncing in the direction in which it was thrown. 3. Next, throw an underhand pass with backspin. You and the players will notice that the ball will bounce and probably go straight up in the air and land a second time in the same spot, and keep on bouncing in that spot until it stops. This is a fairly clear illustration of what backspin can do for a shot. If the ball hits the rim, the backspin will stop its forward motion and possibly cause it to bounce up and fall through the hoop. If it doesn't go in at least the rebound will be close to the basket, where one of the offensive players may tip it in.
	iv Follow-through	1. Any golfer or baseball player will tell you of the importance of follow-through. A player who is going to be a successful shooter must follow through until arm and fingers are straight. 2. Do not allow players to form the bad habit of shortening their follow-through and stopping the shooting motion before their arm is straightened. This voluntary stopping of the shooting motion cannot be duplicated exactly, time after time after time. There will be shots where a player follows through a little more or a little less, and doesn't stop the shooting motion exactly at the same spot every time. 3. A player will be much more consistent by simply allowing the forearm to stop when the elbow forces it to, that is, when the arm is fully straightened. 4. After shooting, a player should come down in position to rebound.
b) Free throw	During a game, players may be awarded free throws which count one point each and are taken from the line at the head of the key, 3.6 meters (15 feet) from the basket. Any type of shot may be used.	1. Ninety-five percent of all players use the one-hand set shot for their free throw. 2. While it is important to remember that the shot must be taken within 5 seconds of receiving the ball from the referee, each player should adopt a consistent pattern for each shot. Some players bounce the ball once or twice, set their hand position, focus on the hoop, take a deep breath to relax, and shoot.
c) Jump shot	This is merely a variation of the one-hand set shot which incorporates a jump just prior to the shot. Its purpose is to raise the shooter above the defense so the shot may not be blocked.	1. The jump should be closely linked with the shot so that the momentum generated by the legs can be transferred to the ball. The action should be in one movement. 2. Much older stronger players can jump, hesitate a moment, and then shoot. This is most difficult and young players should be discouraged from attempting it.
d) Turn-around jump shot	This shot is the jump shot preceded by a pivot.	1. This shot is most frequently used by players in the low post position. 2. Before shooting, the player must be squarely facing the basket.

SKILL	DESCRIPTION	TEACHING TECHNIQUES AND OBSERVATION POINTS
e) Hook shot	This is a variation of the lay-up, where the ball is swung to the side and then over the head so as to avoid the extended arms of the defender.	1. Bigger players should be encouraged to learn this shot with both the right and left hands. 2. Upon completing the shot, players should face the basket squarely in case of a rebound.

SKILL	DESCRIPTION	TEACHING TECHNIQUES AND OBSERVATION POINTS
f) The lay-up shot	Many experts believe that the lay-up is the foundation on which all other shots are based. It is a short shot that usually results from a pass or dribble. It is characterized by a one-foot take off and a short shot with the opposite hand.	1. A player who jumps with the left leg will shoot with the right hand. Players should be urged to master the shot with either hand and in games to use the hand that is furthest from the defense, affording less chance of a blocked shot. 2. Players should learn the lay-up in three stages: walking, running and running while dribbling. 3. Control is more important than speed. 4. The ball must be held away from the defense. 5. Every lay-up should hit the backboard. 6. Players should accentuate the vertical leap at take-off and let their momentum carry them to the basket. 7. Do not be too critical of traveling violations in the early learning stages. Players will soon pick up the rhythm of dribbling and shooting without violating. 8. The ball must be grasped with two hands until, at the peak of the jump, it is released with one hand. The ball should be taken as close to the hoop as possible.
g) Variations of the lay-up	**i** Baseline lay-up	1. Usually this requires the player to dribble with the hand closest to the baseline and to shoot with the other hand, gently laying the ball off the backboard.
	ii Underhand and overhand lay-up	1. The underhand lay-up is like the continuation of the softball pitch. The ball is carried lower and lifted toward the basket. 2. The overhand lay-up is carried higher and pushed toward the basket. The overhand lay-up seems to be more successful when the shooter is closely guarded.
	iii Reverse lay-up	1. Sometimes a player is forced to go past the basket before shooting. With the reverse lay-up a player hooks the ball back over his or her head after dribbling just beyond the hoop.
5. Rebounding	At every level, rebounding is a vital part of good basketball, but it is especially important at the beginner level, where many more shots are missed than made. Beginning players will spend a large part of their	

SKILL	DESCRIPTION	TEACHING TECHNIQUES AND OBSERVATION POINTS
	time rebounding, and need much instruction in this area.	
a) Defensive rebounding	A defensive rebound occurs when the defense recovers a missed goal attempt by the offense. Successful teams usually control a high percentage of these missed attempts, thereby allowing the offensive team only one shot at the basket in most cases. The process of defensive rebounding has three components: 　i Obtaining position 　ii Gaining possession 　iii Releasing the ball to a team mate or "outletting." These components, when combined with an aggressive and determined nature, result in successful rebounding.	1. Any player can be a good rebounder. 2. Encourage aggressive play within the rules.
	I Obtaining position	1. For a defensive player, positioning means not only aligning oneself in a good spot to get the rebound, but preventing the offensive player from getting to the prime rebounding position. This is known as "blocking out." The most common means of blocking is to pivot into the opponent's path. Since offense and defense are usually face to face, this pivot requires the defense to turn his or her back on the offense in such a fashion as to remain between the offensive player and the ball. Once this has been accomplished, the defensive rebounder should be ready for the ball. This ready position is just a variation of the basic athletic position. Elbows should be extended, forearms up, and fingers spread. Some coaches refer to this as the "tree" position, for obvious reasons. 2. Keep the hands up. 3. The offensive player must run either to the defender's right or left in order to get a better rebounding position. The defender should wait a moment after the shot goes up to check in which direction the offensive player is going, and then pivot in that direction. 4. A player may pivot either clockwise or counter-clockwise, once the opponent's direction has been determined. For more detail on this see section on Pivoting. 5. Execute the pivot with the hands moving up into the tree position. 6. When fighting for a position, take into consideration the arc of the shot and its angle to the board.

SKILL	DESCRIPTION	TEACHING TECHNIQUES AND OBSERVATION POINTS
	II Gaining possession	1. Gaining possession is one thing. Maintaining it is another entirely. From the tree position, the player locates the ball, flexes knees, and jumps, timing the leap so as to catch the ball at the peak of the jump. However, there is an opponent right behind the rebounder. The good rebounder takes advantage of this, attempting to catch the ball while moving toward it with arms fully extended and at a 60° angle to the floor. This reduces the chances of an opponent reaching over the top and deflecting the ball. 2. Once the ball is grasped, the player brings it to a position just under the chin, with elbows extended. This is called "chinning" the ball. From here the rebounder either repasses immediately to a team mate, pivots to pass, or dribbles the ball out of the congested area. 3. Rebound with two hands whenever possible. 4. Land on both feet so that a pivot can be executed in either direction. 5. Most rebounds fall one to two meters (4-6 feet) from the basket. Avoid positioning too close to the basket. A player who is too close may have to reach directly overhead or behind the head for the ball. This negates any positional advantage he or she has gained.
	III Outletting	1. This is the process by which the rebounder passes the ball out of the congested key area to a team mate, who may attempt to run a fast break if the opportunity is there. A quick outlet is the key to the running game so many teams like to use. This pass is usually a baseball pass because the distance covered is great. 2. Stress the pivot away from defensive pressure, followed by the left or right-handed baseball pass. 3. Urge players to practice the baseball pass with their weak hand. They will be surprised how quickly they can master its use over a seven to eight meter (20-25 feet) distance. 4. Sometimes it is necessary to dribble out of pressure before passing on. Teach players to recognize the situations where passing is difficult, and to fake the pass and dribble away from pressure. There will be times when the middle will open up, and the rebounder may speed dribble for some distance before passing on. This is acceptable, provided the dribbler can maintain complete control of the ball.
b) Offensive rebounding	An offensive rebound occurs when a team recovers one of its own missed shots. This is a difficult area in the game to master, but some experts say an offensive rebound is as valuable as a steal, because it really should be controlled by the defense, who enjoy initial positional advantage.	1. The rules for positioning are not quite as specific as for a defensive rebounder. The offensive rebounder should try to take the straightest route possible to the basket, but since this lane will usually be occupied by the defense, the rebounder must slice close to the defender and try to establish a position either beside or in front of the defender. 2. Instinct is of greatest value in this facet of the game. 3. Always face the basket, in order to see the opponent and the ball. 4. Watch and learn. Three out of four rebounds carry across the hoop, landing on the side opposite the shooter. This side of the court opposite the shooter is called the weak side; and since most rebounds are grabbed there, teams

SKILL	DESCRIPTION	TEACHING TECHNIQUES AND OBSERVATION POINTS
		should be sure that they place a good rebounder on the weak side. 5. Watch the shots of team mates and opponents, and note the characteristics of arc, etc. Do they use the backboard when they shoot? 6. Total possession of the ball is not always necessary: success is measured in other ways. The offensive rebounder keeps the ball alive by tapping it so that a team mate may gain possession. A good offensive rebounder will always be around the ball, and therefore in a good position to pressure an opponent's outlet pass.
c) Shooting with an offensive rebound		1. Just as in the defensive rebound, two hands on the ball is a must. Quickness is the greatest ally. The ball should be kept high and the shot should be quick. There isn't time to take a deep-knee bend and explode into a two-part jump shot. 2. The backboard should be used on all short shots. Normally, offensive rebounds result in short shots, so be sure to use the backboard.
6. Faking	This is a crucial element in the development of sound passing. It is simply the process of confusing the defense. There are five lanes or routes which passes may take. It is physically impossible for a defender to block all five lanes. However, a quick-handed defender can cover a fairly large territory and make passing difficult.	1. This is where faking comes in. The offensive player who has decided which lane to use can manipulate the defender's arms so that the pass is less likely to be blocked. For example, a player who wishes to use the high lane to the defender's left would fake the bounce pass to induce the defender to lower one arm and then, the instant the arm goes down, would pass the ball through the now-vacated lane. If the defender had not taken the fake and left the hand up high, a clever passer would use the lower lane to throw the bounce pass. Essentially, faking forces a defender to make a commitment to the particular stance or body position. Depending on how that player adjusts, the offense adapts its attack. 2. The best fakes are short and sharp. They are more effective than exaggerated fakes, take less time, and help maintain the player's own balance. The purpose of a fake is to throw the opponent off balance. 3. Fakes should always be directed toward the basket. The pivot foot should always be further from the basket than the other foot. This principle will make all moves positive and aggressive.
7. Specialized Individual Techniques		1. All players playing the perimeter positions should face the hoop at all times. They should avoid moves which would require them to turn their backs on the basket. A player who cannot see the basket is less likely to see an open team mate and more likely to be double-teamed. 2. The following are four moves for perimeter players, all based on a short but aggressive jab step that covers a distance of fourteen to twenty centimeters (6-8 inches). Combined with this move is a sharp downward movement of the ball in the direction of the jab, simulating the first part of a driving or dribbling motion. Post moves will be discussed later.

SKILL	DESCRIPTION	TEACHING TECHNIQUES AND OBSERVATION POINTS
a) Jab and shoot	This first move requires the player to take the jab and then, leaving the jab foot where it is, to rise up and shoot using the jump shot.	1. Weight must be kept over the back foot, the pivot foot, to prevent the player from falling over when the jab step is taken. This is both difficult and important. Players must be made to understand what it means to have one foot step forward, but the weight remain on the back foot. 2. The step must not exceed fourteen to twenty centimeters (6-8 inches), or else the player's weight will shift to the front foot. 3. Ideally, the defensive player will either retreat a step, or lower his or her hands in anticipation of the drive, thus providing the opening for a successful jump or set shot. 4. In the past, many experts have told players to begin from the basic athletic position, fake the drive by jab-stepping at the defense, and then step back and shoot. However, if the weight is kept on the back or pivot foot, there is no need to retrace that initial jab step. Simply rise and shoot the ball. It is for this reason that the player should learn to shoot with feet staggered either way. 5. Players should learn to use either foot as the pivot foot, and be able to shoot with either foot slightly ahead of the other. To do so, will give the offensive player a marked advantage. Unfortunately, many players never learn this, and remain limited to one pivot foot. Most right-handed shooters feel comfortable using their left foot as the pivot foot and seldom develop moves with the right foot as the pivot.
b) Jab and go		1. Suppose the defender were beaten by the jab and shoot. Next time, sure that the offense is going to shoot again, the defender doesn't retreat or lower hands after the initial jab step. The offensive player must read this, and, instead of shooting, extend the jab step to a full stride, plant one foot beyond that of the defender, push the ball out past this foot, and drive to the basket. 2. Emphasize that the offense is reading the defense's reaction or, in this case, lack of reaction. 3. An offensive player who is within shooting range (and no one should attempt a one-on-one move without coming into range) should need only one or two dribbles to score a lay-up. Most players, regardless of size, can reach the basket after one dribble from any of the perimeter positions. 4. An offensive player who is successful in getting past the defense should angle slightly inside to cut off the defense.
c) Jab, fake and go (rocker step)		1. This move begins as the others with the fake drive. A faked shot from the crouched position follows. A defender, particularly one who has seen the offense shoot out of this position before, should rise to defend the shot. The offense, upon seeing the defender rise up, brings the ball back down and extends the jab step from the initial fourteen or twenty centimeters (6-8 inches) to full stride and drives around the defender. The advantage gained in this move is that, while faking the ball up, the offense's center of gravity is kept low and the player is in a much better position to drive around the defender.

SKILL	DESCRIPTION	TEACHING TECHNIQUES AND OBSERVATION POINTS
		2. The offense gains its advantage in this move by faking the shot without rising up. If the offense can fake the defender into raising his or her center of gravity, the door is open for the drive. 3. Ball fakes must be short and sharp. 4. Players must realize that this move is only successful if they can read the defense's reactions. If the defense does *not* rise up after the fake shot, then the offense must seize the opportunity to continue the jump shot action.
d) Jab and crossover	The previous three moves are all executed on the side of the jab step. Obviously, the player could use either foot as the pivot foot. The jab and crossover counters an over-play by the defense. If the offense jabs with the right foot and prompts, not just a step back but a shift to the offense's right, then the offense can pick up the jab foot and plant it just outside the defense's right foot.	1. Players are more likely to violate the "steps" rule when executing the crossover move. Instructors must pay careful attention to see that the pivot foot remains anchored until the ball begins its downward move on the dribble. 2. In all four of these moves the offensive player has the advantage of having a definite purpose in mind. However, if the defense has superior speed then it is less likely the offensive player will be successful.

C. Individual Defensive Skills

In the game of basketball, teams are expected to score frequently. Therein lies much of the game's appeal. Consequently, sound defensive skills are necessary if the team wishes to limit, but certainly not eliminate, an opponent's shots.

Every player must learn to play competent defense when guarding the ball. Each player should be able to guard an opponent who has all three options— the pass, the shot, and the dribble— or one whose options have been limited.

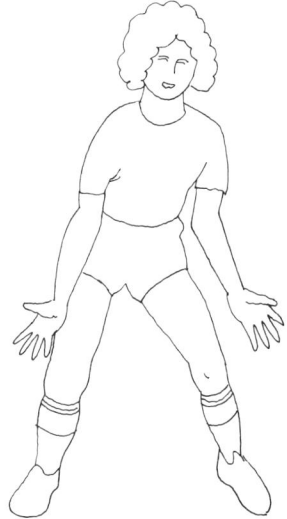

1. Stance	The defensive stance is simply a variation of the basic athletic position.	1. The hands are positioned depending on where the offensive player is located on the court. 2. If the player with the ball is in shooting position, one hand should be up to pressure the shot, and one hand down to protect against the dribble.

SKILL	DESCRIPTION	TEACHING TECHNIQUES AND OBSERVATION POINTS
		3. If the offensive player is dribbling, generally both of the defender's hands are below the waist with the palms up. 4. Once the player has stopped dribbling, the defender may raise both arms high, stepping closer in an attempt to prevent a shot or pass. 5. Keep back straight. 6. Knees should be bent. 7. Hand and arm position appropriate to floor position of player with the ball.
2. Footwork	Balance is very important to successful defense. Players must endeavor to keep the broad base of the basic athletic position even when moving sideways. To do so, requires a series of short jumps.	1. A player's feet should not cross when moving sideways. 2. The distance between the player's feet should change as little as possible. 3. The instructor should make it clear that this technique is used when aggressively guarding the ball.
3. Defending the Man With the Ball		
a) Defending the triple threat player	Any player who is within shooting range and has not used the dribble is considered a triple-threat player.	1. The options of shooting, passing or dribbling are still open. In this case, the defender must keep one hand up to pressure a possible shot or high pass. The other hand should be low with the palm up, to pressure a dribble or a bounce pass. These hand positions can be interchanged, to try to confuse the offense. 2. Depending on floor position and the strengths of the offensive player, the defender may adjust body position to try to force the offense one way. For example, an offensive forward should never be permitted to drive to the basket along the baseline. The defender may wish to over-play to that side slightly, to ensure that it doesn't happen. If an offensive player is particularly strong driving in one direction, the defender may compensate slightly for that. 3. Even though the offensive player is stationary, it is a good idea for the defense to keep feet moving in anticipation of a quick start by the offense. 4. Learn to recognize and ignore fakes. Never jump to pressure a shot unless the offensive player has done so first.
b) Defending the dribbler		1. The first experience most players have with this aspect of one-on-one defense is when an opponent is advancing the ball up court against full court man-to-man pressure. 2. The dribbler will be too far from the basket to shoot, and, hopefully, all team mates will be guarded closely to eliminate the passing options. 3. The player guarding the dribbler should adjust the basic athletic position so that hands are below waist level, with palms up.

SKILL	DESCRIPTION	TEACHING TECHNIQUES AND OBSERVATION POINTS
	1. Try to make the offense use up as much time as possible. Where teams are limited by a 30-second clock, this is a particular advantage.	1. Nose on the ball. When the ball is in the back court, the line from the ball to the defender's nose should be parallel to the sideline. When the ball is in the front court, the line should be straight from ball to nose to basket. 2. Force the dribbler to change direction as often as possible. 3. Force the dribbler to use the weaker dribbling hand. 4. Play as close as your quickness will permit. At worst, defenders should be close enough to eliminate the crossover dribble. 5. Defenders must stay as low as possible and try not to cross their feet.
	2. Try to steal the ball	1. Always go for the ball as it is rising off the bounce. 2. Any attempt to steal should come from an upward motion of the hands. 3. Try to steal only with the outside hand. If the dribbler is moving to the defender's left, then the left hand should be used. 4. Never attempt to steal unless the body is first in proper defensive position. A foul often occurs when a player tries to steal as a means of recovering from poor defensive position. 5. Be balanced; never lunge. Be prepared to resume defensive play if the attempt is unsuccessful.
	3. Try to lead the offensive player into a particular area of the floor for a double team. A double team is when two defenders guard the player with the ball in an attempt to steal the ball, force a bad pass, or cause a jump ball (see page 36).	1. Here a player must over-play one side, forcing the offense to take a particular route up court. 2. This is a most difficult maneuver, and requires great quickness and anticipation on the defender's part. *Note:* The points mentioned above apply any time the offense is beyond shooting range and has had all passing options reduced.
c) Defending a dead dribble	Any player who has dribbled, stopped but retained the ball, has "killed" the dribble.	1. There is a great temptation here for defenders to get as close to the offense as possible, rise up on their toes, and put both hands as high in the air as possible to prevent a shot. The motivation for this is good: don't let the offense shoot. But it isn't necessary to be so aggressive to prevent a shot. 2. To be sure, a player should step closer, but with one hand up, not two. The closer the defense is, the easier a bounce pass is. One hand should be low to stop the low pass. 3. A defender on tiptoes with arms extended, is liable to be beaten by a give-and-go if the offense does manage to get a pass up. Always be in a position to make a quick recovery or adjustment.

SKILL	DESCRIPTION	TEACHING TECHNIQUES AND OBSERVATION POINTS
4. Defending the Man Without the Ball	Guarding players who don't have the ball will be covered extensively in the section titled Team Defensive Tactics —Man-to-Man	

D. Team Play

1. It is important to remember that it is at this stage that players really begin to play basketball. Preceding skills have been the foundation blocks which enable a player to function in a team situation. Do not presume, however, that a player who has mastered these individual skills will be able to integrate them effectively into a team environment. Players must be constantly reminded, during the individual skills learning process, that basketball is a team game. Therefore, they should be exposed to these team situations from the earliest stages.
2. All basketball practices of Physical Education classes should in some way involve players in team play beginning with the very first day. It needn't always be a full five-on-five scrimmage. It may be best to work up to that by beginning with two or three players per team.

SKILL	DESCRIPTION	TEACHING TECHNIQUES AND OBSERVATION POINTS
1. Team Offensive Tactics — Man-to-Man	Man-to-man offensive tactics are effective against man-to-man defense. However when the defending team uses zone defense, the team with the ball must adjust their strategy to meet this (see Zone Offense).	
a) Two-on-two	A large part of basketball scoring plays are generated by two players working together. For this reason it is important that players be given the opportunity to explore all the possibilities that can result from a two-on-two.	1. All of these two-on-two tactics can be taught by pairing players up and matching them against other pairs. Under the instructor's eye they should try to execute all the moves from every position on the floor. 2. A successful approach is to teach offense before teaching defense. This tends to build confidence in the offense who, for the first while anyway, can run their plays against less-than-perfect defense.
i The give and go	This move requires the offensive player to pass the ball to a team mate and then quickly cut between his or her own check and the ball on a path to the basket, accepting the return pass and attempting to score. The offensive must cut in order to be between the ball and the checking	1. This move can be run by any two players anywhere on the court. It requires simply a pass, followed by a quick cut. 2. A variation of this occurs when the defense, having been beaten once or twice by this move, jumps into the gap between the ball and the cutter to try to steal or discourage the pass. In fact, this is the accepted defensive tactic for stopping the give and go (see Team Defensive Tactics). A smart passer will see that the defender is now vulnerable to an overhead lob pass. 3. A further variation occurs if the give and go doesn't require the initial pass. It is sound offensive strategy, any

| SKILL | DESCRIPTION | TEACHING TECHNIQUES AND OBSERVATION POINTS |

| | player, thereby creating the opportunity for the return pass. | time the defense is playing too close to a player without the ball, for that player to cut toward the basket in hopes of catching a pass. This could be called the give and go minus the give.
4. In a full five-on-five situation, players must be aware of all their team mates so that two players don't cut to the same spot. |

ii The return hand off

Instead of passing and cutting to the hoop, as in the give and go, a player passes to a team mate, follows the ball, and is handed the ball while cutting close to the team mate. This is called a return hand off.

1. In some respects the return hand off is a combination of the give and go and the screen and roll (see below).
2. Once the player received the hand off, the options are the same as in the screen and roll: take the hand off and shoot immediately or drive to the basket aware of any team mate who may be rolling toward the basket as well.

iii Back door play

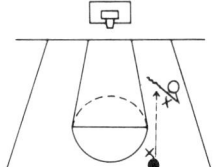

1. From time to time the defense will play so close to their opponents that a pass cannot easily be made. This usually occurs on passes between perimeter players. The player being pressured should move away from the basket drawing the defender away too and then quickly cut to the basket looking for a pass.
2. The key here is to stretch the defense as far as possible before breaking to the hoop.

iv The screen and roll

This practice is referred to as screening (or blocking) *on* the ball as opposed to *away* from the ball which will be discussed in the section on three-on-three.

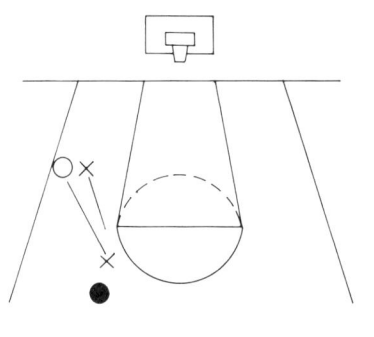

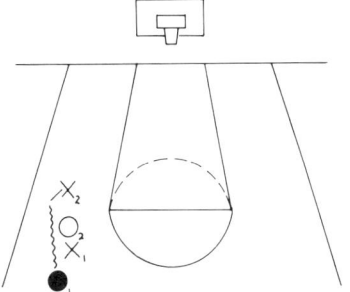

1. The play begins with a team mate of the player with the ball standing squarely beside or behind the defender guarding the ball. This technique is called screening or setting a screen. Best results occur when the screener's shoulders form a 90° angle with the expected path of the dribbler. The dribbler will attempt to move past the team mate's block without permitting the checking player to slip between. In many cases, the dribbler will then be free either to shoot a jump shot or to continue to the basket for a lay-up.
2. However, most teams will use a switch in these circumstances, where the player guarding the screener will jump out to check the dribbler.
3. Here is where the roll comes in. If the screen has been properly executed, the defender, in an attempt to stay with the dribbler, will run into the chest of the screener. At this point (just after contact) the screener should turn toward the dribbler, who will now have passed by, and begin running toward the basket. Since the defenders have switched checks and the player guarding the screener is now behind the screener in a poor defensive position, there could be an opportunity to pass the ball to the screener. The nice thing about the screen and roll is that the screener who unselfishly set a screen for a team mate often ends up with the basket, due to an ineffective switch.
4. The rules governing screening require the screener to be either in the vision of the defender being screened or, if not in the line of vision, a distance of one meter (about three feet) behind the defender. This is to allow the

Note: See page 7 for explanation of key area.

SKILL	DESCRIPTION	TEACHING TECHNIQUES AND OBSERVATION POINTS
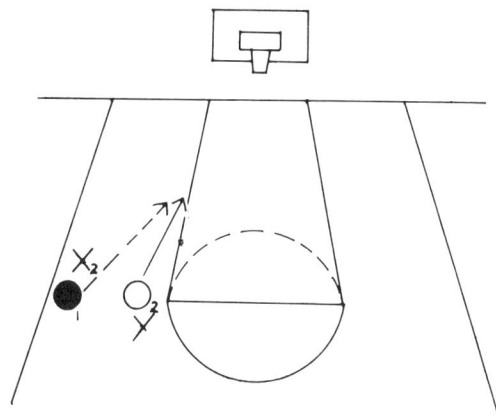		defender a chance to reach to a blind screen. 5. Here, as in all aspects of the game, the dribbler must read the reactions of the defense as to whether to (a) continue the drive for a lay-up, (b) pull up behind the screen for a jump shot, or (c) look to pass the ball to the rolling screener. 6. To avoid an offensive foul for a moving screen, the screener must be stationary before the defender makes contact. It is the dribbler's responsibility to wait until the screen is set and then dribble so close to it as to cause the defender to either stop or hit the screener. Sometimes the dribbler must fake in the opposite direction before beginning to drive, so that this will occur. 7. The screener must roll in order to see the dribbler at all times and be prepared to receive a pass. 8. The screener will roll the instant the dribbler passes and must expect the pass from then on.
b) Three-on-three 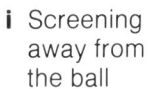	The next step in teaching offense is to add a third player to both sides. All the two-man plays are applicable as well as a few more. Although three-on-three is given as a Level II activity, Level I players should be given the opportunity to experiment informally with three-player games.	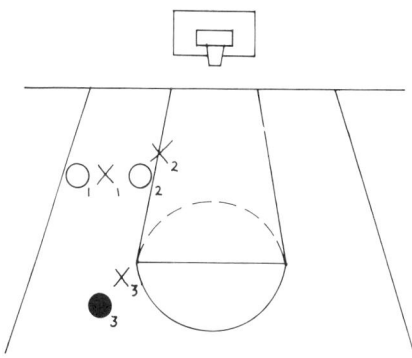
i Screening away from the ball 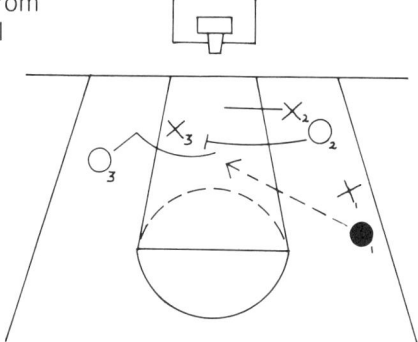		1. This involves a screen and roll between two team mates when the ball is held by a third team mate. 2. The movements of the screener and cutter are almost exactly the same as those of the dribbler and screener in the two-on-two play. However, rather than the screener planting and waiting for the cutter to run the defender into the screen, the screener seeks out the defender and sets the screen as close as possible to that player. 3. Many current offenses rely heavily on this type of screening, reasoning that more players are involved when the screens are away from the ball and more of the court is occupied. For example, when one player has the ball, there can be two screens and cuts being executed by the other four offensive players.
ii The post game 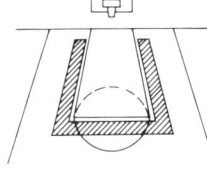	Penetration is a necessary part of every offense, and is achieved by the dribble and the pass. It is very difficult to master an aggressive drive to the basket which can result in a lay-up or jump shot, or a pass to an open team mate.	1. Most often these passes are to the post player, usually called "the post," who is positioned somewhere along the key from the block to the foul line. This post player, or center, is generally one of the tallest players, who will normally play with back to the basket, as opposed to the perimeter players who most often face the basket. 2. A player is referred to as a "high post" when standing at the free throw line.

SKILL	DESCRIPTION	TEACHING TECHNIQUES AND OBSERVATION POINTS
	In fact, most teams are fortunate if they have one player who can do this consistently. That leaves the pass as the weapon that most teams must use to get the ball near the basket. 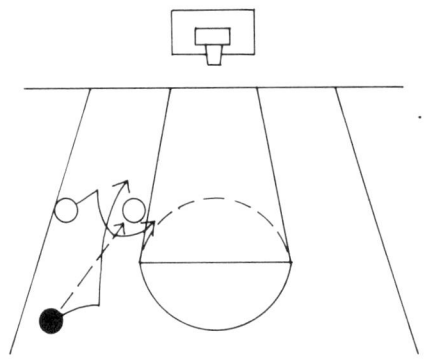	3. A "low post" stands closer to the basket on either side of the key area. 4. Usually the post game is a three-man game, with a guard and a forward on the side of the post. They will pass the ball among themselves, forcing the defensive post to change positions frequently. (See Guarding the Post, page 41.) When an opportunity arises the ball is passed to the post. 5. Once the ball is passed to the post, the post can take advantage of poor defensive position and either drive to the basket or shoot immediately. 6. The passer can cut to the basket in hopes of a return pass (give and go). 7. Either the guard or the forward can set a screen for the other, perimeter player, who will cut and receive the ball from the post. 8. The two perimeter players may "x" or "scissor" the post. The passer will always go first to avoid confusion. The center may hand the ball to either player. 9. The post can fake the ball to the perimeter players and then shoot or drive to the basket. 10. As you can see, the possibilities are limited only by the initiative and creativity of the players.
c) Five-on-five— Principles		1. Full team offense is the most challenging part of the game to execute and to teach. For this reason there are a number of prevalent theories on how it should be played. Some feel that teams should be equipped with set patterns, not unlike a football team. Others feel the players should be taught principles which govern their reactions on offense. Their play would be considerably less structured than the "patterned" teams, with more room for creativity. 2. Basketball is a fluid game which constantly confronts its players with different alignments and player configurations, requiring them to adjust, react, and improvise. The term "freelance" has been applied to this style and, while it is accurate to a degree, it gives the impression that all five players are operating independently. This should not be so. The following are the principles that should govern team play. 3. Although it is unlikely that Level I and Level II players will be able to grasp all the principles and techniques of the full game, they should be permitted to play as often as possible.
i Positional play	The five players should be positioned so that the floor is balanced. Balance is necessary to spread the defense out and prevent it from clustering in one area. It stands to reason that the defense is weakest when it is forced	There are different ways of achieving and maintaining floor balance. An instructor may tell the players: 1. There are five positions on the floor that must be occupied. Which player plays where is unimportant. This situation could apply to a team with five players of similar height, quickness, and skill level. 2. Each position has a specific position to occupy - right forward, left guard, low post, etc. 3. One or two players must play specific positions, such as

SKILL	DESCRIPTION	TEACHING TECHNIQUES AND OBSERVATION POINTS

to cover the greatest area. Below are diagrams of some common offensive alignments.

point guard or high post, and the others should take the remaining positions, but are not each assigned to a specific one.

4. These instructions, and there are endless combinations and variations of them, should result from a careful analysis of the players' strengths and weaknesses, and how best these qualities would assist the team effort.

5. If a team uses a 1-3-1 alignment with two post players and three perimeter players, it may have one post player who is a very good ball handler and outside shooter. It may be to the team's advantage to have that person play some of the time from a perimeter position. The instructor, therefore, would tell that player to use personal judgment as to where to line up, and instruct the perimeter player to be ready to fill the post spot when the other player vacates it, so that the 1-3-1 alignment is maintained. The other post player due to particular limitations, size etc. may be told not to leave the post spot under any circumstances.

6. Rebounding is another good reason for offensive floor balance. Since offensive rebounds are so crucial, a team must see that it occupies as many likely spots where a missed shot may fall as it can. The three best rebounders should form a triangle of rebounding power in front and on either side of the basket. The fourth player, usually a guard, stands between the foul line and the broken line. The fifth player, usually the smaller of the guards, plays back as a safety against the fast break. This balanced position gives the offense a good chance at retrieving a missed shot or slowing the opponents' fast break.

ii Shot selection

The most important thing a player must learn is what constitutes a good scoring opportunity. There are several questions that must be answered before the shooter can make the decision to shoot or not to shoot.
- What is the score?
- Is the team protecting a lead, or trying to come back?
- How much time remains in the period or game?
- Is there a team mate with a better scoring opportunity?
- Is the shooter within range, that area within which there is a reasonable chance of scoring?

A six-meter jump shot may be appropriate in one set of circumstances but a critical error in another.

1. Players will learn only if they get healthy doses of game-like scrimmages which will incorporate all the factors referred to in these questions (listed in the adjacent column).

2. Another factor that develops from shot selection is scoring balance. Instructors should develop offenses that generate an equal number of scoring opportunities for all five players or all five positions over the season.

3. This does not mean that all five players will necessarily take the same number of shots, or score the same number of points. It is exceedingly rare that a team would have such even scoring distribution.

4. Almost always, one or two players will consistently score more points than the others. Although this is not desirable it is no disaster either. The rest of the team will realize that the high scoring averages result not from a lop-sided offensive attack engineered by the instructor, but from the fact that these players take better advantage of the situations in which they find themselves.

5. Here are some reasons for implementing an offense that creates scoring opportunities for all:
   a) Teams whose offenses are geared to one or two players are easier to defend, because it's easier to predict who will shoot.
   b) The philosophy of team play is better served by this

SKILL	DESCRIPTION	TEACHING TECHNIQUES AND OBSERVATION POINTS
	The ability to distinguish a proper shot from a poor one comes with experience and correction.	approach than by the "star" system. A balanced scoring attack encourages unselfish play. c) Injuries and foul trouble become less serious.

iii Ball movement	Consistent offensive play demands rapid ball movement from inside to outside and from sideline to sideline. This forces the defense to adjust its position continually.	1. Since the defense has little difficulty keeping up to the ball when it is being dribbled, players should be urged to pass the ball whenever possible.
		2. It is physically impossible to keep up with a sharply thrown pass, and a series of quick passes can put enormous pressure on the defense.
		3. It is a player's responsibility always to expect a pass and to be in position to receive it. Players should always be maneuvering their defenders for this purpose.
		4. The dribble should really only be used for the following:
		   a) To advance the ball up court if a pass is not possible.
		   b) To make an aggressive drive to the basket.
		   c) To improve a passing angle.
		   d) To escape from a crowded area.

iv Conditioning and timing	Players must be in top physical condition to play the game well. This type of conditioning is best achieved by doing drills that contain the actions they will be expected to perform in a game. This makes it easier for the instructor to disguise conditioning as learning.	1. Players can gain considerable confidence in their performance if they believe that they are in better condition than their opponents. It is up to the instructor to find some way to prove this to the players. 2. Players must be allowed the practice time to work together, so as to learn the rhythms and moves of their team mates. A certain familiarity will develop that permits players to anticipate each other's reactions to good effect.
d) Building the half court offense		1. After reflecting on the preceding principles and evaluating the players, an instructor is ready to teach a plan of attack to the players. Confidence is crucial. The instructor who is not completely sold on the plan will transmit doubts to the players, whose performance will suffer. This requires considerable research and preparation. In this section, I will not use a specific offense, but, rather, mention teaching methods and strategies as they apply to any offensive alignment. 2. The first step is to present the players with a picture of the finished product. As an architect convinces clients with scale models and detailed drawings, so, too, must the players be sold with a total picture of the offense and its suitability for their purposes. Once the players understand the goal for which they are aiming, they will be more receptive to learning it piece by piece.

i Two-on-two	Players should now be permitted to explore the many offensive movements that can be generated by two team mates, and the many	1. Once all players have experimented sufficiently with the give and go, the screen and roll, etc. from the guard forward positions, the instructor may have them line up in any of these positions:
		   a) Forward and low post
		   b) Forward and high post

SKILL	DESCRIPTION	TEACHING TECHNIQUES AND OBSERVATION POINTS

	different ways these two can generate a score. To create the realism of a guard forward play, the players may not be permitted to cross the imaginary line running from basket to basket. In effect, they are playing on half the court. Play must remain on the side of the court on which it begins.	c) Guard and high post
		d) Guard and guard
		2. Generally the play should begin with a perimeter player, guard or forward, holding the ball. Obviously, the instructor should assign positions based on the offensive alignment planned for the whole team (1-3-1, 2-1-2 or 1-2-2). The ones I have arbitrarily chosen are from a 2-1-2 alignment where the post player may start high or low.
		3. Instructors should restrict the space in which the players may operate so that game-like action will result. It would be unrealistic to permit the Two-on-two Drill to occupy the entire half-court as this wide open environment would never occur in a real game. See Chapter Three, Drills for a detailed description of the Two-on-Two Drill.
		4. It is a good idea for all players to learn to play all positions, for three reasons:
		  a) Injuries, foul troubles and unforeseen circumstances may make positional adjustments necessary somewhere down the road.
		  b) By knowing the general movements that can be expected from each position, players will find it easier to spot open team mates for passes.
		  c) It will broaden the players' general knowledge of the game of basketball, and perhaps prompt them to create situations and ask questions of the instructor that they may not have asked, had they not learned all the positions.

ii Three-on-three	The third position with a defender is added.	1. The combination which the players practice from a 2-1-2 alignment could be:
		  a) Guard, forward, low post; this would be called the strong side game. In any alignment of players, the side on which the post lines up is the strong side because it will have three players. On the weak side are two.
		  b) Guard, guard, forward
		  c) Forward, post, forward
		  d) Guard, guard, high post
		2. See Chapter Three, Drills for a detailed description of the Three-on-Three Drill.

iii Four-on-four	It is not necessary to outline the combinations here. It suffices to say that the floor is becoming more crowded, and the instructor should be emphasizing floor balance, quick accurate passing, unselfish team play, and balanced rebound strength.	
iv Half-court scrimmage (five-on-five)	All positions are occupied. This level will have been	1. In the early stages, it is important that players be observed as closely as possible, so that errors can be corrected

SKILL	DESCRIPTION	TEACHING TECHNIQUES AND OBSERVATION POINTS
	reached slowly, so that players will have become aware of where they should be as plays develop, and where their team mates are likely to be.	before repetition has reinforced them. 2. Players must be urged to rebound every mis-shot aggressively, until either the offense scores or the defense gains control. 3. Situations may occur where all offensive players are not actively involved in the play. If a screen and roll is being run by two players, that leaves up to three offensive players who are not involved. Yet their actions are crucial to the success of the screen and roll. They must keep their checks occupied by cutting and moving so that these defenders are not free to interfere with the play and so that they themselves will be available for a pass if the play is unsuccessful. There is a trend among coaches today to discourage the screen and roll because it is difficult for all three players to keep their defenders busy without getting in the way of the two-man play. However, players will work hard at keeping defenders occupied if their play is noticed. While it is necessary to criticize errors, it is more important to praise good play. Compliment good play away from the ball. 4. Obtain films or videotapes and watch the players not directly involved in the play. How do their movements contribute to the play's success? 5. Praise the play makers. 6. By using the score clock, put teams in situations where the time remaining and the score will affect their shot selection. A short game of three minutes which begins with the score tied, or with one team ahead by a few points, is made very exciting and realistic if the clock is used. This forces the players to think of the rules, strategy, fouls, and so on, all those aspects of the game which seldom come into play when teams scrimmage.

e) Special situations		1. There are only three ways that the ball can be put into play:
		    i) a pass from out of bounds
		    ii) a jump ball
		    iii) a missed free throw
		2. Every player should feel comfortable in each of these situations.

i The pass from out of bounds	A pass from out of bounds may result from an opponent's score or a violation or foul by an opponent.	1. Unlike soccer, the player may pass with one or both hands, provided the invisible plane rising from the out of bounds line is not broken by any part of the player's body. The pass must be thrown within 5 seconds. 2. The real responsibility for successful in-bounds passing lies not with the passer but with the passer's team mates. They must make sharp cuts so that they will be open as they move toward the ball, not away from it. This may require a screen away from the ball so that one player will shake free.
ii Jump ball	A jump ball will occur at the start of a half or	1. Timing for the jumper, and player deployment around the circle, are the two important factors. If a player has a

SKILL	DESCRIPTION	TEACHING TECHNIQUES AND OBSERVATION POINTS
	quarter, when two opponents hold the ball simultaneously, or when a ball goes out of bounds and the referee cannot tell who was last to touch it. The team that can control jump balls plays with a distinct advantage. At least four jumps will occur during every game, which could easily result in four shots for the team that controls them. With a 50% shooting average, these four shots yield four points.	better than average chance of winning the tap, the tallest team mate should be at the side of the circle to which the jumper can most easily tap the ball. This will be at the east or west spots, as opposed to north or south. The two quickest players should be on north and south, with one in position to break for a pass and lay-up should the tap be won, and the other ready to guard against a fast break by the opposition if the ball is lost. 2. If circumstances dictate that a player is unlikely to win a jump ball, team mates should try to anticipate a play by the opponents and line up in defense against it. Usually the guard nearest the defensive basket should line up a few steps off the circle, so as not to be beaten by a long pass.

iii Free throw attempts	1. Free throw attempts are awarded when:
	  - a player is fouled in the act of shooting
	  - a technical foul occurs
	  - a team exceeds the limit of team fouls in one half
	2. Free throw attempts are taken from a line at the end of the key, 4.6 meters (15 ft.) from the basket.
		1. Lack of concentration and preparation result in many missed free throws falling into the hands of the offense. See the diagram for the allotment of spaces along the key. The defense should be sure that all four of their spots are occupied, and that one of the two players nearer the shooter is responsible for cutting the shooter off and catching the rebound. The fifth defender should line up behind the inside defender on either side, but must remember to indicate this position to a rebounding team mate so that a loose ball can be tipped in that direction. The important thing to remember is that all five defensive players should be as close to the hoop as possible.
		2. The offensive team should have two players in the designated spots, a player as far back on the court as the deepest defender, and a third rebounder in a position similar to the fifth defender, one to two meters outside the key and available for a tip from a team mate.
		3. Since the inside defender generally has the advantage on most rebounds, it makes sense for the best offensive rebounder to line up alongside the weaker of the two defenders. To line up next to the better of the two rebounders would virtually eliminate any chance of getting the rebound.

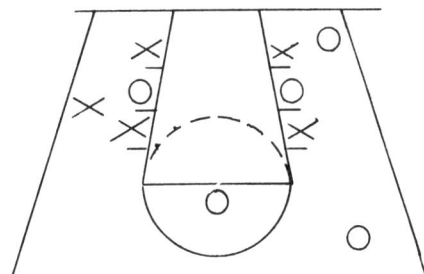

2. Team Offensive Tactics - Zone		1. When a defending team adopts a zone defense, many of the strategies for man-to-man offense are ineffective (see Team Defensive Tactics—Zone). Since the defensive players in a zone react to the ball rather than to specific offensive players, the principles applied by the offense must be different. 2. Beginning players should not be encouraged to play a zone game.
a) Principles		
	i Rapid ball movement	1. Pass the ball rapidly around the perimeter. 2. The offense can tire a zone defense by using this tactic. Over the course of a game, some defenders may not be

Note: See page 7 for explanation of key area.

SKILL	DESCRIPTION	TEACHING TECHNIQUES AND OBSERVATION POINTS
		able to keep up with the ball and will allow scoring opportunities.
	ii Team alignment	1. Defenders in a zone generally adopt specific alignments (2-1-2, 2-3, 1-3-1). Offensive players must realize this alignment and position themselves in the gaps of the zone. See diagram. 2. This is a complex activity, and instructors who feel their players are ready to attempt zone play should equip themselves with a detailed coaching manual (see Appendix I).
	iii Quick transition	1. If the offense can get the ball up court *before* the zone has a chance to get into position, then the chances of scoring are greater.
	iv Penetration	1. By positioning a player on the high post or low post and passing the ball to that player from time to time, the zone will be forced to shrink in size as it collapses on the ball. The post player then returns the ball to a perimeter player who should be able to shoot unobstructed.
3. Team Defensive Tactics—Man to-Man		
a) Principles		1. At one time, man-to-man defense allocated the responsibility of guarding specific opponents to specific players on the team. Player A on Team X had to try to stop Player B on Team Y; and at the end of the game it was determined who played the best defense by seeing how few points Player A allowed Player B to score. The theory was great, but it soon became obvious that it is next to impossible to stop any player one-on-one. Even an inferior player can score in a one-on-one situation with some degree of consistency. 2. Defensive theory changed to include zone defense, which will be discussed later, and ultimately to the current concept of man-to-man defense, which makes each individual responsible for a player *and* the ball. All five players are reacting to their check and the ball every time either moves. It has become a player's responsibility to be ready to help out when a team mate is beaten. The goals have shifted from stopping individuals to stopping the ball. This theory is much more consistent with the philosophy of team play and cooperation that should characterize the game.
	i Floor position	1. There is an easy way to determine where on the floor a player should be. An imaginary line runs between the ball and the player's check. This is called "the line of the ball." This forms the base of a triangle of which the defender is

SKILL	DESCRIPTION	TEACHING TECHNIQUES AND OBSERVATION POINTS

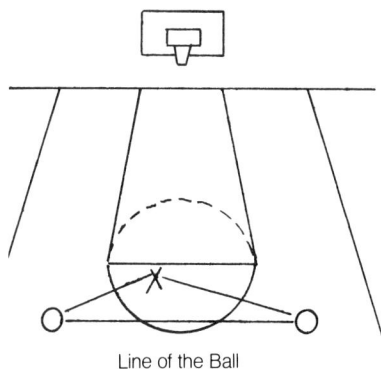

Line of the Ball

the apex. It is a flat triangle, because the defender should be only a step off the line of the ball, a step toward the basket.
2. Defensive players must at all times see both their checks and the ball, and be between their opponents and the ball.
3. This section discusses floor position mainly as it applies to perimeter players. A separate section (see page 41) deals with defending against post players.
4. The greater the distance between the ball and the player, the more the defender can "sag" toward the ball.
5. Defenders should keep the hand nearest the ball in the passing lane, that is, above the line of the ball, so as to discourage a firm pass. The only pass that should be permitted is a high lob pass which, in most cases, will be slow enough to allow the defender to be in a good defensive position when it arrives.

ii Communication

1. Good defense depends on communication from player to player. The simplest aspect of man-to-man defense, who is guarding whom, can easily break down and result in a flood of opposition lay-ups. Every substitution must be noted, and appropriate adjustments made.
2. One can never be too careful, or check too frequently.
3. The player guarding the ball must be told what's behind him or her. Is there a high post? a screen left? Has the forward cleared out for a one-on-one move? As long as the talk is related to player position or movement, there can never be too much talk on the court.

iii Transition

1. This is the period immediately following a change in possession. Many feel that the best teams are those which make this change quickest.
2. Once a team loses possession, it must immediately sprint back, locate individual checks, and be ready to play defense before the ball arrives.
3. Players must be set up before the ball arrives, not as it arrives.

iv Ball side, help side

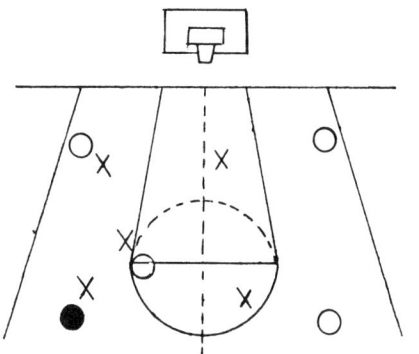

1. Some coaches use these terms to identify the defensive players who are in a better position to help out. The ball side is the side of the court where the ball is, and the other side is the help side, as divided by the imaginary line down the middle of the court.
2. Defenders on the ball side should be guarding their checks fairly closely to try to prevent their movement into good scoring position.
3. Those on the help side should be looking for opportunities to help their team mates, should they be beaten by their check. Help side players must also be aware of the players they are guarding, who may be trying to move into scoring position themselves.

SKILL	DESCRIPTION	TEACHING TECHNIQUES AND OBSERVATION POINTS
b) Two-on-two		
i Defending the give and go	As mentioned in the team offense section (see page 37), the success of this tactic depends on the cutter getting between the guard and the ball. To take this tactic away, players must follow this simple rule: as soon as the ball is passed "jump to the ball." There should be no hesitation.	1. The defender who jumps in the direction of the pass will be occupying the area through which the cutter must go. In most cases the cutter will then change direction and look for the lob pass over the defender's head. 2. Once this cut occurs, the defender must maintain the defensive position mentioned earlier, that is, between the ball and the player one step off the line of the ball, watching the ball and the player. 3. Generally the lob pass is very hard to complete in a five-on-five situation, because there are other defenders sagging in to help out from the other side.
ii Defending the screen and roll		1. There are five ways to defend this tactic, all of which have value and all of which have a place in the basketball team's defensive strategy. 2. The key ingredient to all of these is communication between the team mates. Defenders must talk to each other and help each other out. The players guarding the ball must know well in advance that a block is coming. 3. It is the responsibility of the player guarding the screener to shout out, loud and clear, that a screen is coming on the right or left side. Once this has been established, the defenders fight the switch in the appropriate fashion.
	1. Slide through	1. If the screen has been set beyond the shooting range of the ball handler, then the defenders may execute the slide through, which permits the player guarding the ball to step behind the player who is screening and pick up the dribbler on the other side. 2. It is easy to see why this is not an acceptable tactic when the dribbler is within shooting range: it would be easy to simply step behind the screen and shoot a jump shot.
	2. Jump switch	1. The player guarding the screener jumps out from behind the screen directly into the path of the dribbler while shouting: "Switch!" to a team mate. 2. Both feet must be firmly planted before any contact occurs, or else the player will be charged with a foul. The objective is, at best, to draw a charging foul and, at worst, to force the dribbler to stop the dribble and pick up the ball. 3. Meanwhile, the player who was originally guarding the dribbler will allow the screener to begin a roll to the hoop, and then step between the screener and the ball, hoping either to steal a low pass or to force a high lob pass that can be intercepted by help side players.
	3. Over play	1. The player guarding the ball who knows there is a screen to the right will simply step up on top of the screen in the path which the dribbler ordinarily would take. 2. This forces the dribbler to go the other way, away from the screen. This is particularly useful if the screen is set for a strong hand dribble. 3. Some players do not drive nearly as well with their weak

SKILL	DESCRIPTION	TEACHING TECHNIQUES AND OBSERVATION POINTS
		hand. Obviously, a player who uses this tactic must be prepared to react quickly to a drive the other way.
	4. Help and recover	1. This is a much more subtle tactic. It is predicated on forcing the dribbler to hesitate, which will allow the defender guarding the dribbler to get over the screen and back into a good defensive position. The player guarding the screener blocks a jump switch by stepping out from behind the screen. 2. At best, the dribbler will stop dribbling, and will be recaptured by the original check, while the other two players will remain together. 3. At worst, the dribbler will retain the dribble, but be forced to go wide, thus allowing the checking player to get over the block and back into position. 4. For this tactic to work, the offense must be setting good, solid screens and the dribbler must be making a real effort to cut closely to the screen. Many screen and roll plays are not set perfectly, and there is often considerable space between the screen and the dribbler, thereby permitting the defender to slip through and avoid the need for a jump switch, or help and recover maneuver. Players should be encouraged to try to fight through, or fight over, these screens whenever possible, and these maneuvers should only be used in the event of a very good, solid screen.
c) Three-on-three		
i Defending the screen away	There are really only two ways to defend this offensive maneuver	1. Switching is out; there is no need. 2. The defender being blocked can go either above or below the screen. In order to choose, the defender must look at the ball and judge where the cutter can be most dangerous, and then take the shortest route, above or below, to that spot. 3. Since most screens away are on help side defenders, it is to the defender's advantage to "sag" into the key when a 3 second count will be put on the offensive player.
d) Guarding the post 	The post position is any position occupied around the perimeter of the key. The post player's back is generally kept to the basket, and this poses some unique defensive problems. There are four positions that the defensive post player can use: 1. directly behind the post position 2. in front of the post position between the ball and the post player	1. The first two of these can create problems. Playing directly in front makes the defender helpless against the lob pass. Playing behind makes the penetrating pass to the post player too easy. A good pass is extremely dangerous, for the post player can get the ball at will. A simple rule is to straddle on the base line side when the ball is below the foul line extended, and to straddle the post position on the high side if the ball is above the foul line extended. 2. When the post player is in the lower half of the key, the defender should step in front of the post player when the ball crosses the foul line extended. If the post player is in the top half of the key, or along the foul line, the defender should step behind the post player when changing from side to side. 3. Once the post player has the ball, defense is very difficult.

| SKILL | DESCRIPTION | TEACHING TECHNIQUES AND OBSERVATION POINTS |

3. straddle the post position on the base line side
4. straddle the post position on the high side

Defenders must try to keep their feet on the ground, and to attempt to block a shot only when directly in front of the shooter. When a player has been beaten and tries to recover by blocking the shot, it invariably results in a foul. In this case, try only to pressure or distract the shooter and then, after the shooter has released the ball, be sure to prevent the shooter from getting the rebound. A good rule of thumb, when beaten near the basket, is to put the hands straight up, jump straight up only after the shooter has left the ground, and concentrate on blocking out.

4. Good post defense is not preventing the score once the ball has penetrated, but rather, preventing the penetration in the first place.

4. Team Defensive Tactics—Zone

a) Principles

Although no attempt will be made to analyze zone defense in detail, it is certainly worthwhile to take a look at the principles and possible motivations for its use.

1. Briefly, zone defense assigns each player to an area of the court. Each defender is responsible for guarding the offensive player in that area.
2. These areas or zones fluctuate somewhat in size depending upon the location of the ball. Generally speaking, zones try to protect the basket first and then cover the perimeter positions.

There are numerous reasons for using a zone defense.

3. Larger players can remain near the basket so as to be in a good rebounding position.
4. There is less movement by the defenders therefore less likelihood of fouling.
5. If a team is quick to set up its zone, the offense is forced to set up a more deliberate style which is time consuming.
6. A compact zone defense discourages dribble penetration and forces the offense to shoot from the outside.
7. If one or two players are weak defensively, they can be "hidden" in a zone, although it should be remembered that a good zone defense is usually comprised of five players who have sound man-to-man defensive skills.
8. An unusually talented opponent can be neutralized to some degree with a zone.

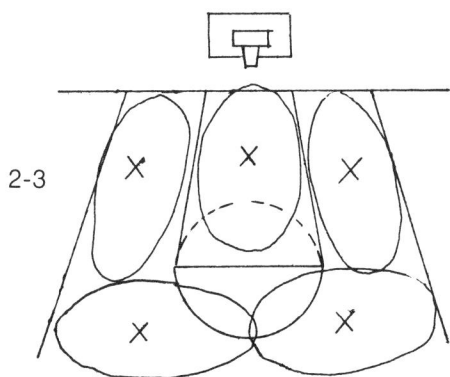

2-3

b) Zone alignments

1-3-1

1. There are a number of different zone configurations, the most popular of which are the 2-1-2, the 2-3, the 1-2-2, and the 1-3-1.
2. Zones fall into two large categories, passive and aggressive zones. Passive zones are concerned mainly with protecting the basket against penetration. They often are vulnerable to quick perimeter passing and accurate outside shooting.
3. Aggressive zones attack the ball wherever it is, sometimes with two players. This is known as double-teaming. Defenders frequently gamble at intercepting passes.
4. A poised and well-prepared offense can take advantage of double teams on the perimeter to get uncontested close shots. However, if the offense is the least bit

SKILL	DESCRIPTION	TEACHING TECHNIQUES AND OBSERVATION POINTS
		hesitant an aggressive defense like this can be devastating.
		5. Aggressive zones are often extended to three-quarter or full court. To extend the defense beyond the half-court area is called pressing. If the ball is contested right from the in-bounds pass after a basket, this is called a full-court press. Until twenty years ago the press was generally reserved for late in the game as a catch-up tactic. However, today it is not at all unusual to see teams pressing all game long.
		6. There is a wide variety of presses that are divided into man-to-man and zone. The use of the press makes basketball infinitely more exciting because of its gambling nature. The more territory a defense must cover, the easier it should be for the offense to score, but this is often proved wrong by a quick, gambling, pressing team.
E. Rules	It would be redundant to devote a large amount of space to a thorough treatment of the rules of the game, particularly when local modifications exist for different leagues. The official rule book and referee's case book are both available at a nominal cost from the B.C. Amateur Basketball Association—the address is given in the Appendix—or directly from most local associations. This section is limited to a few general comments on the rules.	Note: The section on the rules has been based on the F.I.B.A. rules developed by the International Federation of Amateur Basketball. There may be some variation between the rules outlined in this section and those played in various areas. The local Basketball Officials Association can be of assistance in clarifying and interpreting the rules.
a) Control of the ball		1. The ball is to be held and played with the hands. 2. It may be passed, shot or dribbled, but to strike the ball with the fist or foot is a violation resulting in loss of possession.
b) Ball-into play	The ball can be brought into play in only three ways:	1. A jump ball 2. A pass from out of bounds 3. A missed free throw
c) Ball out of bounds	The ball is out of bounds when:	1. It contacts the floor, any person or object beyond the inside edge of the boundary line. Boundary lines, therefore, are out of bounds. 2. It contacts a player who is either on or beyond the boundary line. 3. It contacts the ceiling or basket supports. The player who last touches the ball is considered responsible for causing the ball to go out of bounds.
d) Progression with the ball		1. A player may not move while carrying the ball. 2. A player may pivot with the ball (see page 18), but must

SKILL	DESCRIPTION	TEACHING TECHNIQUES AND OBSERVATION POINTS
		either pass, shoot, or begin to dribble before the pivot foot is moved. 3. The ball can be advanced by dribbling, bouncing the ball with one hand. 4. The dribbler may not dribble with two hands at once. Once the ball has come to rest on one or both hands, the player may not resume dribbling. 5. A player who is closely guarded may not hold the ball for more than five seconds. Should he do so, a jump ball would result.
e) Time restrictions		1. Offensive players may not be in the key area for more than 3 seconds. Defenders have no time limits. 2. The offensive team must advance the ball across the mid-court line within 10 seconds of gaining possession. 3. A player may only hold the basketball for five seconds. 4. A team must shoot within 30 seconds of gaining possession. 5. A pass from out of bounds must be thrown within 5 seconds.

F. Officiating

| | There is much more to officiating than simply knowing the rules of the game. In fact, the rules are only one of the three areas in which officials should be trained:
1. rules
2. the philosophy of officiating, and
3. the mechanics or methods of rule application. | 1. **Rules:** These have been outlined in Section E.
2. **Philosophy:** The purpose of having officials at all is to see that no player gains an advantage through misuse of the rule. The key word, obviously, is "advantage." Officials should look first for rule infraction, and, second, to see if the rule breaker has gained an advantage. Only then should a whistle be blown. Inexperienced players make numerous rule infractions, but often gain no advantage. Hence, it isn't necessary to charge them with a foul or violation, although their transgressions may certainly be mentioned in hopes they can learn their skills properly. Officials should also be urged to understand the intent and spirit of the rules, as well as their literal meaning. This will make any use of judgment or discretion all the more accurate.
3. **Mechanics:** Included in this area are floor position, hand signals, and division of responsibilities between officials. Also very important is the skill of administering jump balls, which occur a minimum of four times in a game, though there are often many more. Every time a whistle is blown, a signal should follow. The rule book has diagrams of the universally accepted hand signals. They should be practiced, so that they will become an automatic reaction. These can be practiced as a large group, with the leader making an imaginary call and each group member responding with the proper signals.
   a) *Lead and trail officials:* One official should always be ahead of the play (lead), and the other should be slightly behind the play (trail). If a turnover occurs, their responsibilities shift: lead becomes trail, and trail becomes lead. The officials are on opposite sides of |

SKILL	DESCRIPTION	TEACHING TECHNIQUES AND OBSERVATION POINTS
		the imaginary line running between the baskets. On out of bounds calls, each official takes the sideline nearest him. The lead official covers the baseline, and the trail official has the mid-court line for back court violations. The lead official is responsible for 3 seconds in the key. The trail official must watch the ball as it advances up court, and call dribble or 10-second violations. Officials should change positions every so often, so that one official does not end up being lead official all the game at one end of the floor. The defensive team could get very irritated if one official called all the fouls against them, simply because that official was under their defensive basket most of the time. b) *Pre-game conference:* The two officials should meet before the game to discuss some or all of the following: division of the floor; floor mechanics (example: when to change from trail to lead; most officials change after every violation or foul): basic rule situations; and special situations, such as how to cover a full court press, and so on. Officials are also expected to monitor the following time limits: 3 seconds in a key, 5 seconds for a throw in, 5 seconds for a free throw, 5 seconds for a held ball, and 10 seconds to advance the ball across the center line. With the exception of three in the key, the seconds should be indicated by a slight flick of the wrist and a mental "one thousand one, one thousand two," etc. This should be practiced against a clock to ensure maximum accuracy. In conclusion, remember that the players and spectators are there for a keen competition, not to be entertained by two individuals with whistles. Officials must, by their unobtrusiveness and calm demeanor, create an environment in which players can perform at their best. Information on the the training of student officials is available from the B.C. School Sports Federation located at 1200 Hornby, Vancouver, B.C. V6Z 2E2.

Chapter Three
Drills

A. Basic Skills

1. Free Movement, Change of Direction

Using the control dribble, players move randomly around the court, changing direction when they feel comfortable, employing either the crossover or the reverse dribble. It is important that the players feel no pressure from external variables, such as a defender, or a coach's whistle, that would impair their concentration. Depending on the space you have to use, and the number of players, you may wish to reduce the area used after a time, so that the players must be aware of, and cautious of, other players.

Learning Outcomes

1. Players develop a familiarity with the ball.
2. Players must become aware of those moving around them.
3. Players develop their skills at the crossover and reverse dribbles and changing of direction.

2. Partner Shadow

Players are scattered in pairs randomly around the floor. One player is designated as the leader, and the other becomes the shadow. The shadow attempts to stay one meter behind the leader as the leader tries to dodge and cut and shake free. This is an excellent drill for footwork, and can also be applied to ball handling by giving both the leader and the shadow a basketball. The instructor may wish to handicap the players in this shadow drill. For example, the leader may have a basketball and the shadow may not. The leader may be dribbling two basketballs if particularly proficient - the shadow, only one.

B. Passing Drills

1. Box drill

Four players, one of whom has a ball, make a five-meter (about 15 foot) square. Three other players stand within the bounds of that square. The four players are team mates, as are the three within the square. The object for the team of four is to complete as many passes in a row as they can. The three players in the square will try to prevent that. Of the three, one must always be closely guarding the ball, as it would be unfair to leave the ball unguarded and then have the other three players go and stand in front of the other three offensive players. The four offensive players can be given specific tasks: such as - of every ten passes, three must be diagonal passes. A simple rotation can be worked out where, after every ten passes, or after every interception or deflection, players alternate spots so that each of the seven players has a turn in each of the four offensive spots and three turns as a defensive player. The four corners of the box may be marked with tape. Offensive players would then be required to keep one foot on the tape so the square does not grow larger.

Learning Outcomes

1. Players develop their ability to fake the ball.
2. "Passing through traffic" becomes easier.
3. Players become familiar with their reactions of opponents to fakes.
4. Players realize that they must be alert for a pass at any time.
5. Players have an opportunity to practice their passing and receiving technique.
6. Players begin to realize the value of anticipation from an offensive and defensive point of view.

2. Fake, fake, fake!

Two players stand three to five meters (10-15 feet) apart. One player has a ball in the basic athletic position and the other stands with arms folded. The player with the ball starts the drill by either passing or faking a pass. The partner must catch the ball if it is thrown or keep arms folded if it is a fake. A point is awarded to the receiver if the ball is caught, and to the passer if the receiver reacts to the fake or drops the ball. The purpose of this drill is to help passers realize the effectiveness of their fakes. The passer is limited to three fakes before the ball must be passed. A gap between players may be widened or lessened if the game becomes too easy or too difficult.

Learning Outcomes

1. Players begin to realize whether their fakes are effective or not.
2. Players develop their reactions.

3. Pig in the Middle

This drill will help the passer get the ball past the person guarding. Each group of three players has one ball and designates one player as "the pig" who is stationed between the other two, but must stand closer to the player with the ball. The player with the ball has three seconds, counted by the defender as: "thousand one, thousand two," etc., to release the ball. If the passer is unsuccessful, either by reason of deflection, interception or hesitation, the passer goes to the middle. Players must execute short, sharp fakes. Players may not throw high lob passes, nor are the receivers permitted to move from their spots to catch the ball.

Learning Outcomes

1. Players become comfortable passing under pressure.
2. Players realize how they can maneuver a defender by faking the ball.
3. Players learn how to defend against a passer who cannot dribble.
4. Players become familiar with the passing lanes.

4. Two-player Technique Perfection Drill

With one ball for two players, the group pairs up and executes the four basic passes: chest pass, bounce pass, overhead, and baseball pass. Players stand from three to five meters (10-15 feet) apart.

Learning Outcomes

1. Players develop their passing and receiving skills.
2. Players have an opportunity to concentrate on technique without there being any defensive pressure.

5. Turnaround

Partners stand four to five meters (12-15 feet) apart. One player stands with back to the ball. The passer throws the ball while calling out the partner's name. As soon as the receiver hears the call, he or she turns and attempts to catch the ball. This promotes a quick hand-and-eye reaction. Once the receiver can easily handle the pass in the shooting zone, waist to neck, passes should be varied - some good passes, some bad - so that the receiver becomes used to reacting to all sorts of passes.

Learning Outcomes

1. Players develop quick hand-eye reactions.

6. Keep Away

This drill stresses accurate passing, sure-handed receiving, and intelligent movement of the ball. At least four players will be required, but as many as twelve to fourteen could be used. The rules are simple: no dribbling, no shooting. How long can one team maintain possession of the ball? Players can hold the ball for only two seconds. The player guarding the ball must pressure it, may not sag off, and may not double team a potential receiver. The playing area should be restricted to half-court, and perhaps even smaller if there are only four players. This drill also stresses the skill of pivoting.

Learning Outcomes

1. Players develop the ability to catch and release quickly.
2. Players learn to keep all corners of the court occupied so that the defense is spread.
3. Players learn how to cut and move to get open.
4. Players learn how to set blocks away from the ball.
5. Players learn to be balanced when in control of the ball.

6. Players become more familiar with passing and pivoting.

7. Pass and Pivot Relay Drill

The group is divided into teams of six, which are evenly spaced across the baseline. Each team then spreads itself out in a straight line from baseline to baseline, with a player standing on each baseline. The first player of each team has a group of five or six basketballs. Each team should have the same number of basketballs. On the signal, the first player picks up a ball, pivots, and chest passes to the next player in line, who in turn catches, pivots and passes, and the ball is relayed up the floor to the other end. As soon as the first ball has been passed, the first player immediately turns and picks up the second ball, and the chain begins again. The initial goal is to get all six balls to the other end of the court. Once they are there, the person on that baseline picks up a ball and begins the process again, returning the six balls to the other end. The first team that gets all six basketballs down to the opposite baseline and then back again is the winner. Emphasize proper passing, receiving, and pivoting. The players may be instructed to use only a certain pass each time, e.g. bounce pass, or two-hand overhead passes. It will also be fairly easy to determine the degree of mental alertness of the players in the group.

Learning Outcomes

1. Players develop quick reactions.
2. Players improve their ability to pivot.
3. Players improve their ability to execute the basic passes.
4. Players improve their hand-eye coordination.

8. Circle Passing Drill

Divide the players into groups of five and have them space themselves evenly around any of the jump circles on the court. One ball will be given to each group. Quick passes should be made diagonally across the circle - chest pass, bounce pass, overhead pass, and the baseball pass can all be practiced. Players may not pass to the person on their immediate right or left. To encourage players to evaluate and react to situations before passing, have two balls passed within the circle at the same time.

9. Bull in the Ring

One player stands in the center of either the foul circle or the center circle. Five others stand around the circle with their toes on the circle line. The ball is passed around the circle in an attempt to prevent the player in the middle from deflecting the ball. Players on the circle may not pass to the players immediately adjacent to them. If the ball is touched by the player in the middle the passer takes that spot.

10. Shell Drill

Up to a dozen players can be used in this drill. Six offensive players are designated to occupy perimeter positions. Six defenders guard them. The ball is, at first, slowly passed around the perimeter. The defenders must adjust their positions in accordance with the man-to-man defensive principles. The instructor should initially check each defender's position after each pass.

The ball can be passed more quickly as players become more familiar with their responsibilities. The defenders should be concerned only with their proper position, not deflecting or interrupting the pass.

11. Baseball Pass Drill

Players stand in line along the baseline. The first player in line dribbles out to the free throw line, comes to a stride or jump stop, pivots and chest or bounce passes the ball to the next player in line. Upon doing so, the player turns and runs toward the basket at the other end of the court looking over his or her inside shoulder. The player who receives the chest or bounce pass dribbles to the free throw line and then throws a baseball pass to player number one. Player number one receives the ball and scores the lay-up. The passer, once the ball has been thrown, breaks into a sprint in an attempt to catch the lay-up as it comes through the net before it hits the ground. These two players execute the same drill coming back to the basket from which they started.

C. Dribbling and Footwork Drills

1. Check Control Dribbling Drill

Choose an area large enough so that players have freedom of movement. Have the players spread themselves randomly around this area. Twenty-five players could fit fairly comfortably in half to two-thirds of a full court. Each player has a ball. At the instructor's signal, players begin dribbling, and attempting to check the ball from any of the other players with their free hands. A player who loses control of the ball, either by mishandling or due to the check of another player, must take the basketball and begin circling the court, dribbling with his or her weak hand. The drill continues until one player remains dribbling on the court. As players are knocked out, the drill area should be reduced by the instructor so that the final two competitors are in one of the three jump circles.

Learning Outcomes

1. Players become comfortable moving around the court while dribbling the ball.
2. Players develop their alertness to the movement of others.
3. Players learn how to protect the basketball from the opponent.

2. Dribble Tag

Players are randomly spaced in the bounded area, half-court or full court. One or more players is designated "it." On the instructor's signal, that person tries to tag as many players as possible. All players are dribbling basketballs. A player who is tagged becomes "it" as well, until only one player is left untagged, and that player is the winner. Players should be using a control dribble that permits frequent change of direction. Successful players will be able to see what's happening around them, as well as control the ball.

Learning Outcomes

Same as the Check Control Dribbling Drill.

3. Speed and Control Dribble Relays

Instructors should structure different types of relay games to reinforce the need for efficient ball control. Straight ahead shuttle relays are good for the speed dribble, while obstacle courses may be good for the control dribble. Use cones, chairs, or preferably, stationary players as obstacles to dribble around. The players, who must remain stationary, are free to try to deflect the ball with their hands as the players pass.

Learning Outcomes

1. Players learn how to protect the basketball from opponents.
2. Players begin to realize the priority of control over speed.

4. Stop and Go Drill

On the first whistle, players begin running and dribbling, but on the second whistle they must halt but keep dribbling by executing either a stride or jump stop. On the third whistle, they resume running and dribbling. Players should execute stops and starts as indicated in the section on Basic Skills.

Learning Outcomes

Same as for the previous drill.

5. Line Dribble

Players follow the floor markings, changing directions when they come to an intersection. Players may use crossover or reverse dribble.

6. Zigzag Drill

Players in single file zigzag between the sideline and the imaginary center line running from basket to basket. At each change of direction they change hands, executing either a reverse dribble or a crossover dribble. Obviously, as they dribble across the floor to their right, they would be dribbling with their right hand, and dribbling with their left as they return.

D. Dribbling and Ball Handling Drills

1. Dribble Catch

Players perform this drill in pairs. Each has a basketball, and there is a small rubber ball or bean bag for each pair. Players face each other in the basic athletic position and dribble the ball in a control style with their strong hands. As they dribble the ball, they toss the small rubber ball or bean bag back and forth with their weak hands. This forces the players to concentrate on something other than the ball they are dribbling. As they become more proficient, they may wish to try the drill as they walk down the court. Some pairs may even wish to try it with two small balls. Players may have an easier time with this drill if it is first done on their knees, thus permitting them to handle the basketball more easily.

Learning Outcomes

1. Players develop the ability to control the ball without thinking about it.
2. Players become proficient at dribbling with both hands.

2. Hand Sensitizer Drill

The ball is slammed from palm to palm. Players should avoid allowing the ball to hit the center of their palm. This action stimulates the hands and fingers and prepares them for more skilful work to come. In a way, it stretches the fingers so that the player has more control over the ball.

3. Dribbling on the Knees

Players should be introduced to dribbling from the kneeling position. The ball travels less distance, and is therefore easier to control. It is particularly useful when teaching dribbling with the weak hand. Very young players may find it useful to sit back on their heels, thus getting even closer to the ground. The change of hands can be introduced in this position. Obviously, when players have mastered dribbling while kneeling, they should try it while standing.

4. Two-hand Dribbling

If you have lots of basketballs, give two to each player until the supply runs out. Players must try to control the two balls at once. Restrict movement initially, then allow the players to roam around, dribbling the two balls. This may be begun on the knees, then continued in the basic athletic position.

5. Straight Line Dribble

Players move in straight lines back and forth across the court, making one crossing using the speed dribble and the next crossing using the control dribble. Players should use both strong and weak hands.

6. Figure Eight Drill

Standing astride, players pass the ball around their legs in a Figure 8 pattern. Once players become expert at this, they may attempt the Figure 8 motion while walking.

7. Around the Body and Legs

Players pass the ball from hand to hand around their waist in a clockwise or counter-clockwise motion. The ball may be raised or lowered, so that it passes around the knees, thighs, chest or head. Players may stand astride and do the drill around one leg. As the players become more proficient, encourage them to make as many revolutions as they can in 30 seconds. Only beginners should be permitted to watch the ball.

8. Reverse Dribble Tag

Players will be scattered randomly around the playing area, which may be half the basketball court. Only one player has a basketball. On the instructor's signal, this player attempts to tag others while dribbling. Players who are tagged run to the sideline and get a basketball from the instructor, and they become chasers. The last player tagged is the winner.

E. Shooting Drills

1. Around the Gym Relay

Use all the baskets available with one ball for each basket. Divide the group into teams with an equal number at each basket. On the starting signal the ball is rolled from the first player in line to the last player in line who upon receipt of the ball dribbles to the basket and scores the lay-up. If successful the player goes onto the next hoop etc. until a goal has been scored in each basket. This first player dribbles to the front of his or her team's line and the ball is passed through the team's legs until the last person gets it and the procedure is repeated. The team to complete this circuit first is judged the winner. If a player misses three consecutive times in any hoop he or she may move on.

2. Two Against the Rebounder

Three players take part in the drill while a fourth player begins with the ball. The fourth player shoots the ball and if the shot is missed the three players compete for the rebound. When one of the players gets possession he or she will try to score while being pressured by the other players. The two-on-one competition lasts until the ball is in the basket, out of bounds or a foul is called. The ball is then given to the fourth player who will shoot again. This drill is played until one of the three rebounders reaches a designated score of 3, 5 or 7 baskets.

3. Rebound Block-Out Drill

Players form two parallel lines, with approximately 1.6 meters (5 feet) in between each player. Each player in line A has a basketball. The first player in the line shoots the ball over the other line (no basket is necessary) and attempts to retrieve it. His or her partner in line B tries to prevent the shooter from retrieving the ball and tries to get the ball. Instructors or coaches should clarify the difference between a front and back pivot at this time. Once the players understand the technique of blocking out, the drill should be moved to a basket where the player with the ball attempts to score and retrieve the ball. The defender must block the shooter out and then try to recover the ball. This drill continues until either player A scores or player B gains possession of the ball.

4. Basket Golf

Nine spots are designated around the basket. These

spots could be the markings that already exist on the floor such as hash marks along the key or the intersection of the two lines or they could be spots designated by a piece of tape. "Par" is established by the players so that it reflects the difficulty of the shot. A very close shot may have a par of 1 whereas a shot from the top of the key might have a par of 3. A foursome of players would then go through the nine holes recording their scores and computing whether they finished above or below par.

5. Hot Shot Drill

Five spots are designated on the court with cones or tape. A point value of 1, 2 or 3 points is assigned to each spot based on the difficulty of the shot in that area. A player begins with the ball at one of the spots. A time frame of 30 or 60 seconds begins and the points scored by the player are recorded. Players must get their own rebounds and obey the dribbling rules of basketball when moving from point to point on the floor.

6. Twenty-One Shooting Drill

The group is divided into teams of five or six with two teams placed at each basket. Two spots are located at each basket that are equidistant from the hoop. A ball is given to each team. On the go signal the first player in each line attempts a jump or set shot from the spot. If the shot is successful the shooter's team gets 2 points. If it is not successful the shooter retrieves the ball and dribbles for a lay-up and if scored gives the team 1 point. Team members shoot in sequence until the total of their points reaches twenty-one. The fact that two teams are trying to score at the same basket makes for interesting collisions between balls and players. Players may not impede their opponents or deflect their opponents' ball. Any infraction of this sort would result in two free shots for the opponents. Team members are encouraged to shout out their score as it increases so that both teams know how many points the other team has.

F. Modified Games

1. Platoon Basketball

Three teams of five players each are selected. Each team should be outfitted in different colored "pinnies" or uniform tops. One team in red, one in blue and one in yellow for example. The red team and blue team begin play with a jump ball at center court. The yellow team is on the sidelines at center court. The conventional basketball rules are observed until one team scores. As soon as this happens, the team that is scored upon leaves the court and the team from the sidelines steps on. The team that scored retrieves the ball after it goes through the hoop, steps out of bounds beneath the basket where they scored, and may in-bound the ball immediately and attempt to score at the other end. A premium is placed on the quick reaction of the team on the sideline. Once a basket is scored they must jump on the court immediately and pick up their defensive responsibilities. Play continues until a team scores. Again the team that is scored upon leaves the court and the team on the sidelines comes on.

Learning Outcomes

1. This drill is especially useful for having players talk to each other and confirm the fact that each player has a player to guard.
2. This game is particularly amusing when played by boys who use the shirts and skins method of team identification. The team on the sideline is not sure whether they are going to come on the court as shirts or skins and invariably have their shirts half on in anticipation of either throwing them on totally or discarding them.
3. This game is particularly useful when there is only one full court available and anywhere from fifteen to twenty-five players. While the drill was designed for three teams with five members on each team it would be possible to run platoon basketball with four or five teams. Each time a team is scored they go to the end of the line of teams waiting to come on the court.

2. Guard Ball

This is a variation of the individual passing drill, pig in the middle. Three teams are selected with the same number of players on each team. Team A and B face each other five meters (about 15 feet) apart. Team C occupies the middle ground between teams A and B. A ball is provided for each player on team A. The players on team A and B then attempt to pass the ball back and forth without team C deflecting or intercepting the ball. Each time team C intercepts a pass that ball is removed from play. Score can be kept by counting the number of completed passes made in two minutes. Every two minutes the teams will rotate so that each team has an opportunity to play in the middle. Another method of scoring would be to record the amount of time it takes to complete five, ten, fifteen or twenty-five passes. Lob passes which would travel higher than eight feet are not permitted.

3. Bucket Ball

A regular sized basketball court is used with an even number of players on each team. There may be anywhere from five to ten players on each team. Two chairs are placed in the middle of each key. A player stands on each chair with either a bucket or basket in hand. Each team will endeavor to throw the ball to their team mate standing on the chair who will try to catch the ball. If the player on the chair falls off the chair in an attempt to catch the ball then the basket does not count. The normal rules of basketball apply although instructors or coaches may deem it worthwhile to restrict dribbling or eliminate it altogether. Whenever dribbling is eliminated a three or four second count should be put on the players holding the ball so they are encouraged to pass the ball as quickly as possible. Any personal foul is penalized by two free throws from about three meters

(10 feet) away from the basket. There are a number of variations of bucket ball which might include tire ball. The rules are the same except that instead of having a player stand on a chair an innertube is suspended from the ceiling and a point is scored when the ball goes through the innertube.

4. One-on-One Drill

The name of this drill is a slight misnomer in that there is a third player who begins with the ball. Player 01 has the ball but is not guarded. This player is not permitted to move but only to pass the ball. Player 02 is guarded by player X1. 02 must make cuts and fakes in order to get into position to recieve the ball from 01. This drill is frequently adapted to eliminate this initial pass when in fact in game situations players must constantly make the effort to get open and get free and merely assuming that a player will be able to get free within shooting distance of the basket is a false assumption. Player 02 must be made to work very hard in order to receive the ball in a position where he or she is a threat to score. If X1 forces 02 to receive the ball beyond the 18 foot mark X1 has done a good defensive job. Upon reception of the ball 02 must square up to the basket and either shoot or begin a one-on-one move to the basket. A shot will require X1 to initially pressure the shot and secondly block out 02's attempts for an offensive rebound. At this point there are a number of options. If X1 gets the rebound he or she may be permitted to attempt an immediate score. Another alternative would be to "outlet" or release the ball back to 02. If 02 gets the offensive rebound, he or she should attempt to score. Many like the idea of permitting either the offensive or defensive player, upon retrieval of the ball, to score. The drill would therefore continue until either 02 or X1 scored, a foul occurred, or the ball went out of bounds. Remaining players should be in line behind 01. The progression of players through this drill would be first in line to 01 to 02 to X1 to the end of the line. It is to the players' and the instructors' advantage to use as many of the baskets as possible and if possible to have only three or four players at each basket. This maximizes each player's competition. A further variation of this drill would permit player 02 to pass the ball back to 01 at any time in order to make a cut without the ball. Player 01 may be positioned anywhere on the court, although it is practical not to permit player 01 to move around the court.

5. Two-on-Two Drill

An imaginary line from basket to center circle divides the basket area in half. The instructor designates two players to take offensive positions (such as guard and forward or guard and high post). Two defenders are also assigned. Remaining players form two lines several steps behind each offensive player.

To ensure that both sides are ready, hand the ball to a defender who must then initiate the drill by handing it to the offense. Players should use one of the two-on-two tactics described in Chapter Two (e.g., give and go, screen and roll, return hand off). Players should continue until the offense scores, the defense gains possession, a foul is called by the instructor, or the ball goes out of bounds. Players should be reminded not to cross the imaginary line.

When play stops, the defenders go to the ends of the lines, the offensive players become the defense, and the first two players in line step up to play offense.

Every player should have at least one opportunity to play both offense and defense at each position.

Learning Outcomes

1. Players will learn to execute two-on-two tactics in a confined area, similar to game conditions.
2. Players can practice offense and defense.

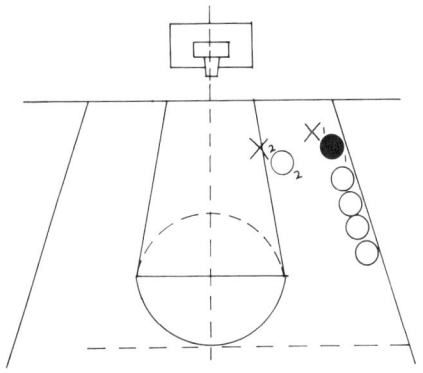

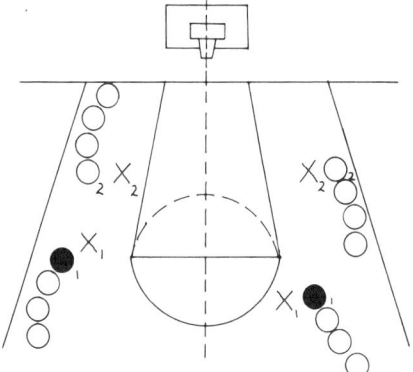

6. Three-on-Three Drill

This drill differs from the two-on-two drill in that two additional players take part so the group should be divided into three lines, and it may not be necessary to restrict the court area. This will depend on which position the instructor wants occupied. A strong side combination of guard, forward and low post may be limited to half the basket area plus the key giving them approximately 60 percent of the basket area to work with.

If two guards and a high post are used, no court restrictions are necessary.

Chapter Four
Sample Lesson Plans

The following sample lesson plans include material mostly concerned with Level I, although references are made to situations where all four levels could, and should, be participating together.

The lesson plans are based on the following framework:

1. Twenty-four pupils per class.
2. Class length of sixty minutes.
3. Equipment - minimum 12 basketballs (or 1 for every 2 people)
   - miscellaneous physical education items such as pinnies, bean bags, whistles, etc.
4. Facility - a full length basketball court with at least two baskets.

Instructors should choose a teaching formation which could be used each time a lesson is taught. A large semi-circle with the instructor at the center is recommended. Players should either stand or be seated and should also be able to get into the alignment quickly. Instructors should prepare a concise explanation and demonstration of the skill to be taught. If the instructor does not feel capable of adaquately demonstrating the skill, a competent player or players should be taught before class to serve as demonstrators. It is important to remember that players learn best by doing.

Lesson One - Rules and Principles of the Game

1. Introduction

Note: This lesson may be used whenever a basketball court is not available. It need not be Lesson One. However, players should be introduced to basic rules early in the course.

Players should be informed of the origin of the game of basketball and the original purpose of its invention. The original objectives as well as the original thirteen rules of the game, as written by Dr. Naismith (see Appendix II), would merit discussion. Some discussion of team sports as opposed to individual sports would be useful.

Some comments should be made on the purpose of the officials: their role is to see that no team or player gains an advantage through the misuse of a rule. The motto of the B.C. Basketball Officials' Association is "the rules are only a guide."

2. Objective

By the end of this lesson players will:

a) Understand the broad rules of the game and why these rules have been stated as they are.
b) Understand more about the dimensions of the court, the ball, the hoop etc.
c) Have learned a little bit about the history of the game of basketball and how it has evolved to its present state.

3. Warm-up

For this lesson, this would be omitted.

4. Review

For Lesson One, this would be omitted.

5. New Material - 50 min.

a) A film on the rules of the game.
b) An explanation of the long term assignments that players may have to do during the course of this unit.
c) An evaluation.
d) Discussion of the rules and officiating section of the book which includes floor position of officials, hand signals, duties of scorers, timers, floor officials.
e) Players should receive a copy of the score sheet with an explanation of how to keep it.
f) General discussion about officiating.
g) Players may discuss things they have noticed regarding the nature of the officials and the job they are supposed to do.

6. Culminating Activity

Remind players that the next class will be in the gymnasium and that they should be dressed appropriately. The topic of that lesson is Passing and Receiving. Include a brief explanation of passing, its value to the game of basketball and why, for example, it is better to pass the ball to a team mate than to dribble the ball oneself, and why quick and accurate passing puts more pressure on the defense than dribbling.

Lesson Two - Passing and Receiving

1. Introduction

Effective team play cannot exist without accurate, frequent passing and confident receiving. In fact, proficiency in these skills can make an otherwise limited player very useful. Although some minimal strength is needed to perform the various passes used, it is not essential that a good passer should be particularly strong. The skills required to be a good passer and receiver are largely mental skills. Historically, the best passers were smaller players who were not as skilful at shooting, scoring and rebounding, but today larger and more talented players are being made aware through good coaching techniques that the key to a successful team is its ability to pass the ball.

2. Objectives

By the end of this lesson players will:

a) Appreciate the value of good passing and receiving.
b) Have learned to execute the basic passes correctly.
c) Have demonstrated the ability to receive the ball comfortably and under control.

3. Warm-up - 5 min.

Introduce players to the value and importance of warming up before exercising. The continual jumping and running involved in basketball tends to put strain on the muscles in the lower part of the back so players should be sure that they are well warmed-up before any activity. If for some reason, activity stops during the lesson and players are inactive for 10 minutes or longer, they should be warmed-up again before taking part in strenuous activity. In succeeding lessons, the instructor may want to incorporate ball handling and skills into the warm-up. This allows players to review what they may have learned previously by repetition during the warm-up.

Initially, players should be led through a 3 to 4 minute stretching routine before the lesson begins.

4. Review - 5 min.

During the stretching routine, the instructor should ask questions of various players pertaining to the discussion on the rules of officiating on the previous day.

5. New Material - 25 min.

a) Demonstrate the three basic passes, chest pass, bounce pass and the two-hand overhead pass.
b) Demonstrate the proper receiving technique.
c) Players do not have basketballs at this time, but they should execute imaginary passes back to the instructor concentrating on proper hand, arm and foot movements.
d) Select one player and demonstrate the following drills:
 - passing in pairs, the Turn-around Receiving Drill, Fake, fake, fake!, Pig in the Middle, and Bull in the Ring.
e) Players should pair off with a ball for each pair and execute the drills on the signal of the instructor. The instructor should circulate around the gymnasium and observe as many pairs as possible before changing the drill.

6. Culminating Activity - 15 min.

Players should return to the teaching configuration where the instructor will comment constructively on what he or she observed.

The instructor will then introduce the Keep Away Drill which will incorporate most of the skills practiced during the previous section.

7. Closing Remarks - 5 min.

Explain that the topic for the next lesson is Footwork and Ball Handling, so reference should be made to some of the important aspects of these skills.

Lesson Three - Footwork and Ball Handling

1. Introduction

Control is the most important word the player will ever hear when being taught the sport of basketball. First learn to control movements - to run, stop and change direction at will - then learn to control the ball while moving.

2. Objectives

By the end of this lesson players will:

a) Have learned the correct body position for stopping, starting and changing direction.
b) Be able to employ these skills in a competitive situation.
c) Have developed some familiarity with controlling the basketball by dribbling.

3. Warm-up - 5 min.

Basic stretching while holding a basketball. If there are not enough basketballs for each player in the class, players should be asked to share a ball with someone else.

4. Review - 10 min.

Players pair off and quickly execute the passing drills learned in the previous lesson, moving very quickly from one drill to the other.

5. New Material - 20 min.

a) Introduce the dribbling and footwork exercises (see drill section) with particular emphasis on shifting body weight, making sure the weight is on the proper foot, and developing the proper backward lean when stopping. The players should play tag, follow the leader and some of those other games that will emphasize proper footwork.
b) Demonstrate the two methods of stopping, the jump stop and the stride stop.
c) Introduce one knee dribbling so that players can get the idea of first, handling the ball without moving, and dribbling the ball while moving, either walking or running and finally either walking or running with

defensive pressure.
d) Introduce Dribble Tag, Dribbling on the Knees, and some of the other games outlined in the drill section.

Note to instructors:

Although in learning dribbling it is usually necessary for a player to practice the skill alone, stress that the skill is never performed in isolation during a game and that a player who is dribbling must constantly be looking for an opportunity to advance the ball by either a pass or a shot.

6. Culminating Activity - 15 min.

Divide the players into teams of three, and introduce the bean bag relays.

Players should be reminded of the dangers of over-dribbling in a game situation and the rest of the class should be devoted to half-court games of three-on-three basketball, with no dribbling permitted.

7. Closing Remarks - 5 min.

Explain that Lesson Four will deal with Shooting, and that the four most important things in shooting are - arc, backspin, follow-through, and confidence.

Lesson Four - Shooting

1. Introduction

This lesson will be broken into two parts. Players will first learn the lay-up shot from both sides of the basket with both their strong and weak hands. Some of the more advanced players may go on to learn some variations of the lay-up such as the reverse lay-up shot. The drill can be done in groups and all players can participate in the drill.

In the second part players will be introduced to the set shot, which advanced players may develop into the jump shot.

2. Objectives

By the end of this lesson players will:

a) Have learned to shoot a lay-up shot with their strong hand.
b) Have learned to shoot a stationary set shot from the broken line.
c) Have a clear understanding of the components of successful shooting.

Warm-up - 5 min.

After a brief stretching period, divide the players into small groups to practice ball handling, passing and receiving skills, as well as the running and dodging skills they have learned in the past few days.

4. Review - 5 min.

Use team oriented drills, that is, relay type drills or passing, dribbling drills that require players to compete in teams.

5. New Material - 20 min.

a) Arrange the players in the teaching semi-circle and demonstrate the lay-up, first using the two-foot parallel position, and then using a jump rope to mark a line at which players must do a jump stop, step over the rope and shoot. Players attempt both. Once players have learned the technique and demonstrated some expertise, divide them into groups at the various baskets. Level I players will continue practicing the conventional lay-up shot, more advanced players adding the variations including practicing shooting with weak hand.
b) Give individual attention to any players who do not grasp the lay-up shot right away, while the rest of the class is practicing.
c) Encourage players to use reciprocal teaching techniques, that is, to analyze the shots and skills of those in their group and make positive comments about the good things, and constructively criticize the errors in their team mates' skill performance.
d) Regroup the players in the teaching semi-circle and demonstrate the set shot, emphasizing arc, backspin, follow-through and confidence. Players will then each have a try shooting one-handed with the ball resting on the palm of their hand. As they become proficient at shooting with one hand, they will be allowed to steady the ball with their other hand.
e) Divide the players into small groups at different baskets and work with those players who still have not mastered the one-hand shot. More proficient shooters can practice alone.

6. Culminating Activity - 20 min.

Introduce a team play drill such as Platoon Basketball.

7. Closing Remarks - 5 min.

Briefly explain one-on-one basketball which will be the topic of the next lesson. Emphasize that one-on-one skills are only valuable if these skills are integrated into a team situation.

Lesson Five - One-on-One Basketball (Offense and Defense)

1. Introduction

Emphasize the importance of being able to play one-on-one basketball, that is to be able to take advantage of a situation where the defender is in a poor position and the player with the ball can make a move to score. By the same token, on the defensive side, to be able to dominate one's opponent is essential to the team's success.

2. Objectives

By the end of this lesson a player will:

a) Understand the three basic one-on-one moves to the basket.
b) Understand the importance of receiving the ball in scoring position.
c) Develop the ability to observe the strengths and weaknesses of individual opponents.

3. Warm-up - 5 min.

Around the Gym Relay.

4. Review - 5 min.

Review basic passing, shooting and footwork skills.

5. New Material - 20 min.

a) With players in the teaching semi-circle, demonstrate the jab and fake. Players will then pair off taking a turn at offense, attempting to execute a convincing fake, and then a turn at being the defender.
b) Players will then return to the teaching semi-circle where the instructor will demonstrate the jab and shoot. Players will again pair off and practice this move.
c) Players then return to the semi-circle where the jab and go is demonstrated. Players pair off and execute this.

6. Culminating Activity - 20 min.

Players are assigned to challenge ladders based on their current level. All Level I players are on the same ladder and they spend the rest of the lesson challenging each other in an attempt to get to the top of the ladder.

7. Closing Remarks - 5 min.

Remind the players of the importance of incorporating one-on-one play into the team play and indicate that the next lesson is two-on-two basketball.

Lesson Six - Two-on-Two Basketball (Multi-Level Lesson)

1. Introduction

Two-on-two basketball serves as a good introduction to passing in team play.

With two-on-two basketball, a player who has the ball will be aware of only one team mate. As additional team mates are added, the capacity to concentrate is taxed to the point that only the very best players can consistently pass to the player who is open.

2. Objectives

By the end of this lesson players will:

a) Understand the function of the screen and roll, and give and go, and other two-on-two scoring maneuvers.
b) Develop the ability to pass under defensive pressure.
c) Develop an appreciation for the clever passing play.

3. Warm-up - 10 min.

After brief stretching players should run through the basic passing drills introduced in earlier lessons: Pig in the Middle, Bull in the Ring and Fake, fake, fake!

4. Review - 5 min.

Ask players to demonstrate the three basic one-on-one moves to the basket.

5. New Material - 15 min.

With the group watching, demonstrate the various methods of scoring with the two-man game. Demonstrate one at a time and then have the players disperse to the various baskets in groups of four and try to use the techniques just demonstrated. Care should be taken in dividing the players up so that Level I players will be playing against each other, Level II against Level II and so on.

6. Culminating Activity - 20 min.

Arrange a two-on-two tournament. Encourage players to use all the two-on-two and one-on-one techniques previously learned. Games should continue until one team has scored five baskets. It may be useful to conduct two or three mini-tournaments so that there is a Level I champion and a Level II champion and a Level III champion. This sort of division can be done with or without the knowledge of the players.

7. Closing Remarks - 5 min.

Remind the players that the lesson for the next day is three-on-three basketball and that they will be expected to apply the one-on-one moves and two-on-two maneuvers during three-on-three basketball.

Lesson Seven - Three-on-Three Basketball

1. Introduction

This is the next step to good team play. Rebounding could be emphasized during this lesson. When playing three-on-three, the teams should maintain court balance which should result in rebounding opportunities.

With the third player on each team, however, there is less need for dribbling. In fact, instructors may choose to eliminate or minimize dribbling during the early stages so that players learn the value of screening away. To set a screen on the ball when the player can't dribble is pointless.

2. Objectives

By the end of this lesson players will:

a) Understand the principle of screening away as it applies to team offense.
b) Understand the importance of court balance as it relates to rebounding and scoring opportunities.
c) Become familiar with the transition play or fast break.

3. Warm-up - 5 min.

Around the Gym Relay.

4. Review - 5 min.

Ask players to explain two-on-two methods of scoring.

5. New Material - 15 min.

a) Three-on-three techniques should be demonstrated one at a time to the group. Players should be reminded that two-on-two and one-on-one techniques can be incorporated into the three-on-three game.
b) Players should practice the Two Against the Rebounder Drill.
c) Another very useful drill to introduce in this lesson is full-court three-on-three, during which players will become familiar with fast break opportunities.

6. Culminating Activity - 25 min.

Keep Away! The 24 players will be divided into four teams of 6 players each. Two games of Keep Away will take place simultaneously in the two half-court areas. If time remains, players may play three-on-three with no dribbling.

7. Closing Remarks - 5 min.

Players should be reminded of the tournament during the tenth lesson and that the eighth and ninth lessons will deal strictly with team offense and defense. The instructor will announce the make-up of the teams that will compete in the tournament.

Lesson Eight - Team Play -Offense

1. Introduction

By this time players should have received sufficient background to understand and execute five-on-five basketball.

2. Objectives

At the end of this lesson players will:

a) Have appreciated the satisfaction of a team working together to produce a basket.
b) Understand how the one-on-one, two-on-two and three-on-three moves are incorporated into full court play.
c) Understand how to contribute to a scoring attempt even when not directly involved in the play.

3. Warm-up - 5 min.

Dribble Tag.

4. Review

For Lesson Eight, this will be omitted to allow more game time.

5. New Material - 25 min.

a) Introduce the five-on-five configuration that will be used by all teams in a scrimmage and tournament play. Explain how the one-on-one, two-on-two and three-on-three moves learned up until this time are incorporated into a five-player offense.
b) Five-member teams should be pre-selected by the instructor to ensure equitable distribution of Level I, Level II etc. players. The same teams will be used in the defensive lesson next and in the concluding tournament.
c) Play should be half-court where each team gets five opportunities to score. Both baskets should be used thereby allowing four teams to play at once. It is recommended that each of the five scoring opportunities begins by passing the ball in from out of bounds.
d) The instructor should be prepared to comment on each attempt to score and indicate whether the offense is applying the principles previously taught. For example, compliment a two-on-two screen and roll that results in a successful basket.

6. Culminating Activity - 20 min.

Each team should be given the opportunity to scrimmage full court, even if this is only for a few minutes. The instructor should restrict his or her comments to the offensive principles discussed during this lesson.

7. Closing Remarks - 5 min.

These remarks might best be delivered before the culmination activity. The instructor should ask the players to give some consideration to how to stop the offensive maneuvers of their opponents. Players should be reminded that the next lesson will deal with team defense and that there may be an opportunity for some of them to learn on their own during the scrimmage situation.

Lesson Nine - Team Play -Defense

1. Introduction

It is unlikely that any team will shoot very well everytime they play, but by playing sound defense and not permitting opponents to shoot easy, unpressured shots, a team can compensate for their own poor shooting. Sound defensive play can add a very consistent component to any team. In most instances defense is a mental skill, one that can be perfected by any athlete.

Levels I, II and III should concentrate only on executing man-to-man defense while Level IV may learn zone defense.

2. Objectives

By the end of the lesson players will:

a) Be able to put consistent aggressive pressure on the ball.
b) Learn to position themselves properly when their check does not have the ball.
c) Be able to anticipate and defend an opponent's scoring opportunities.

3. Warm-up - 5 min.

Zigzag Drill.

4. Review - 5 min.

Review the principles of offensive play.

5. New Material - 30 min.

a) Using the Shell Drill, the instructor teaches defensive player position of those not guarding the ball. The players should be divided into four teams of six with two teams at a basket. The six players on offense should spread themselves around the perimeter and begin the Shell Drill.
b) Using the same teams as in Lesson Eight, players should scrimmage half court with the instructor commenting on the proper or improper defensive positions of the players. Each team should have at least five attempts on offense and five on defense. If time remains, the instructor may organize full-court scrimmages.

6. Culmination Activity - 10 min.

Teams should get together and plan their strategy for the next day. The instructor may answer questions and generally be used as a resource person during this period.

7. Closing Remarks - 5 min.

Before class is dismissed the instructor should distribute the schedule of games for the next meeting and the referee and table official assignments.

Lesson Ten - The Tournament

1. Introduction

This tournament, with minimal input from the instructor, is a wonderful opportunity for players to demonstrate their own initiative and creativity.

2. Objectives

By the end of this lesson players will have:

a) Understood the concept of team competition.
b) Demonstrated the capacity to officiate either at the table or on the floor.
c) Played with sportsmanship, enthusiasm and confidence.

3. Warm-up 3 min.

Teams should be allowed three minutes before each game in order to loosen up.

4. Review

For this lesson, this would be omitted.

5. New Material - 45-50 min.

Games may be measured by time (10 minutes, for example, either running time, where the clock runs continuously for the whole time, or stopped time where the clock stops every time the whistle is blown. or by score (15 points). It is recommended that in order to best duplicate actual game conditions the games should use stopped time with the referees being required to make the appropriate hand signals to signal time in and the table officials to operate the game clock.

The tournament winner can be determined in a variety of ways. The obvious one would be simply to confer the championship title on the team that won the most games. However, the instructor may wish to assign points to the participating teams on the following basis:

- 10 points for a victory
- 5 points for a loss
- a score out of 5 pts. be assigned by an impartial board for sportsmanship
- an additional point for each individual on the team who scored during the game.

This last provision will encourage the teams to provide scoring opportunities for players who might ordinarily occupy supporting roles.

A scoring breakdown of this nature requires even the most hardened win-at-all-costs competitor to think about sportsmanship and team play.

6. Culminating Activity - 5 min.

At the conclusion of the tournament the instructor will comment briefly on the level of play and sportsmanship before conferring congratulations or awards on the successful teams.

Chapter Five
Evaluation

Continuous personal evaluation is a sign of self-discipline and dedication and will be most effective as long as both the immediate and long-term goals are realistic. An instructor may use a combination of subjective and objective evaluation to determine the level of an individual or of the group.

A. Program Evaluation

The success of the program can be judged by the players' response, their progress rate and how much they enjoy playing the game. Their enjoyment may be determined by the extent of participation outside of class time. The number of players who turn out for club or team games, or for tournaments organized outside school hours would be a good indication of success.

B. Player Evaluation

It is important that players be evaluated in three areas:

1. Psychomotor
2. Cognitive
3. Affective

1. Psychomotor

It is recommended that the instructor refer to the activity sequence chart when a player's competence at individual skills is to be evaluated. Check off the appropriate skill when the player has mastered it.

Individual skills can also be tested more formally using skill tests. The following arrangement was worked out by Peter Corby and published in his article "How to Pick 'em" which appeared in *Coaching Review*, Vol. 3, number 16, July/August 1980. It is reproduced with permission.

STATION 1. **Vertical Jump**
On one end of the gymnasium wall inches are marked on athletic tape. Each player will jump and reach as far as he can on the tape markings. Each player has two trials. The best one is recorded. There can be several sub-sections of this station depending on the number of players trying out. This task measures the players' jumping ability and it is a good indicator of one's *anaerobic capacity*. Research has shown that the top basketball player has a high level of anaerobic capacity.

STATION 2. **Dribble Zig Zag**
Here the player must dribble at full speed through 8 cones 4 feet apart for time. Two trials are allowed, with the best one recorded. The player's ability to move with the basketball is strongly related to his ability to perform well in this station.

STATION 3. **Zig Zag Run**
Here the player runs through a zig zag course made by placing four cones 4 feet apart and one in the middle of the square. The player must go through the course as diagrammed in Fig. 2. Two trips of the course make up one run. Two trials are allowed with the fastest one recorded. The success of a player at this station correlates high with his ability to move *without* the basketball which is an important skill of the game.

STATION 4. **Lane Drill**
Here the player starts in the middle of the lane and on command moves quickly to touch the lane lines with his feet. He will go from line to line for 30 seconds. The number of lane lines he touches is recorded. Two trials are allowed. My quickest players over the years have done well here.

STATION 5. **Shooting-Lay-ups**
Here the player will perform lay-ups for 30 seconds alternating from lefthand side to righthand side. Two trials are allowed. The number of lay-ups made are recorded.

STATION 6. **Shooting - Jump shots**
Here the player will shoot 10 shots from three markings around the basket 12 feet away. One mark on the left side, one on the right side and one out front of the basket. Two trials are allowed with the best score out of the 30 shots recorded. I always position myself at this station to observe the shooting technique of each player.

STATION 7. **Shooting Foul Shots**
Here each player will shoot 10 foul shots. Two trials are allowed with both being recorded.

STATION 8. **Speed Pass Drill.**
Here a player will stand 8 feet from the wall and within 30 seconds he will perform as many two hand chest passes as he can. This drill correlates high with the players' passing ability. The number is recorded. Two trials are allowed.

STATION 9. **Defensive Footwork Drill**
At this station players are grouped in even squads of 6. On command players slide sideways, backwards, and forwards in defensive stance. They also stutter their feet, do quick turns and fire out (sprint to end of gym). A general picture can be seen of each player's coordination, balance and agility. These motor skills are essential.

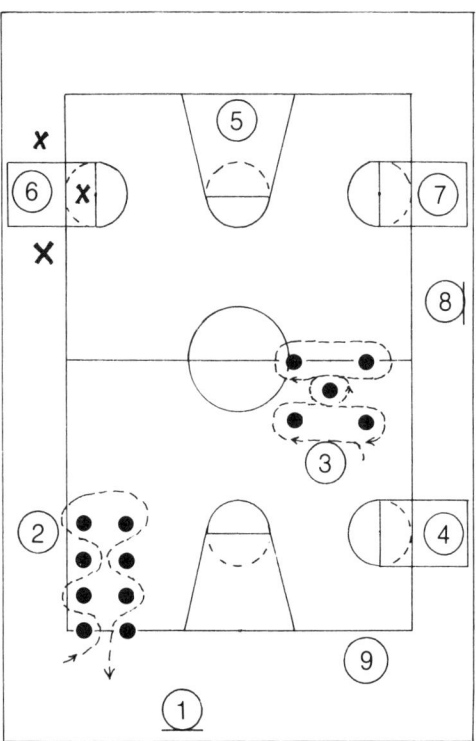

Excellent booklets on basketball skills tests for both boys and girls are also available from the American Alliance for Health, Physical Education and Recreation (AAPHER), 1900 Association Drive, Reston, Virginia 22091, U.S.A. These booklets include detailed information on how to administer the tests and how to use the results to evaluate both players and programs.

Fitness testing is recommended before and after each teaching unit. Basketball is no exception. As mentioned in the introduction to the lesson plans, it is important that players be kept active, that the instructional time be used efficiently to minimize having the players standing around and observing.

Be warned, however, that the mastery of isolated skills does not automatically translate into excellence on the basketball court. During the game or scrimmage, players are frequently faced with decisions as to what skill to use and when to use it. A perfectly-executed chest pass is a mistake if the situation demanded a set shot.

An instructor may be faced with some interesting puzzles when trying to evaluate the players. A highly skilled player who won the one-on-one competition may be a destructive influence in a game because of selfish play. On the other hand, an awkward player who has difficulty with many aspects of the game may, to everyone's surprise, be in the right place at the right time all game long.

Sportsmanship should also be a consideration when evaluating players. A player with a pleasant personality and limited skills who contributes to an enthusiastic and harmonious team atmosphere is an asset to any group and should be evaluated accordingly.

2. Cognitive

Sometimes after the rule and officiating lesson, players should be tested on their ability to interpret the rules. A written test, such as the one below could be used.

TEST FOR REFEREES

Answer *True* or *False*   T   F

1. Basketball rules should be applied from a legalistic point of view rather than from a realistic point of view. ___ ___

2. An official should judge an act in terms of the total situation and the effect any deviation from the exact rule may have on the play. ___ ___

3. It is the intent of the rules of basketball that they shall be interpreted literally. ___ ___

4. The rules of basketball are guides for the intelligent administration of the game. ___ ___

5. The official who desires a rule for every little detail instead of judgment is the superior official. ___ ___

6. The superior official is hypertechnical rather than realistic. ___ ___

7. Officials must rule on anticipation, not on acts completed. ___ ___

8. An official should not under normal circumstances make decisions on any play in front of or near the other official. ___ ___

Answer *Yes* or *No*   Y   N

1. Are there more than three ways to get the ball into play? ___ ___

2. If the ball struck any edge of the backboard top, bottom, or sides would it be legal? ___ ___

3. Where the basket is mentioned in the rules, does that include the net? ___ ___

4. If a player is dribbling the ball and it bounces off his foot and he chases up to continue dribbling, is he still, by the rule, in control of the ball at all times? ___ ___

5. Is it always a violation when the ball comes in contact with a player's foot? ___ ___

6. If a player has been awarded two shots can he take the ball at mid-court for a throw-in, rather than shoot the free throws? ___ ___

7. Does the thirty second clock start only when a team gets control of the ball on the court? ___ ___

8. If two opponents foul each other, the fouls are counted, but are shots taken? ___ ___

9. If a player is fouled intentionally anywhere, at anytime on the court other than when shooting, does he get two shots? ___ ___

10. Do five fouls either personal or technical cause a player to be put out of the game? ___ ___

11. Must a team be in control of the ball continuously without a shot for three seconds, before a player who is standing in the key can violate? ___ ___

12. Can a player be called for traveling or taking steps before he has control of the ball? ___ ___

13. Can a player be called for carrying the ball or double dribbling before he has control of the ball? ___ ___

14. If a player is closely guarded but is bouncing the ball, should a held ball jump be called after five (5) seconds? ___ ___

15. Is overtime a part of the second half in the counting of fouls for the penalty shots? ___ ___

16. Is it the prime responsibility of the lead man to call three seconds in the key?   ___ ___
17. Is it the prime responsibility for the trail official to call back over the center line?   ___ ___
18. If the whistle is securely tied to a lanyard or string around your neck is it necessary to hold the whistle in your hand?   ___ ___
19. Prior to going out on to the court should game, by themselves, and discuss what they will do on the court?   ___ ___
20. If the ball is on the way to the basket on a try and the horn goes for time at that instant, should the basket count if it scores?   ___ ___
21. In counting seconds (key, ten second line, etc.) should the referee count one, two, three, etc.?   ___ ___
22. Would you allow a free shooter more than 5 seconds for a free shot?   ___ ___
23. Should referees *ever* disagree on the court within sight of anyone?   ___ ___
24. Should you signal by a flick of the wrist the three second count in the key?   ___ ___
25. Is it good practice to let a play go if you are not sure of your call?   ___ ___
26. Can a player ask you for and receive a time-out while on the floor?   ___ ___
27. Is it bad practice to hear two whistles on an out of bounds call?   ___ ___
28. Should a trail official coming down court with the ball get too close to the players?   ___ ___
29. Must officials switch position on the court on all fouls and jump balls?   ___ ___
30. If Team A is replacing a player who has committed five fouls, may Team B coach talk to his players at the same time?   ___ ___
31. Should a referee ever be standing still on the court while the ball is in play?   ___ ___
32. Is there a magic spot on the floor where any official should stand with the ball in play?   ___ ___
33. Should both referees watch around the ball at all times?   ___ ___
34. Are the referees responsible for the side line and the end line to their left?   ___ ___

Large assignments should also be included in the evaluation process. Examples of these types of assignments might be:

a) Sportsmanship Project.

A player would attend a tournament or a series of games involving several teams and collect observations on sportsmanship and how it played a part in the games. Examples of the sort of things that players might see would be, the behavior of the coach and players, attitudes of the officials, the effect of the crowd.

   Learning Outcomes

   It is hoped that players will understand that a team which keeps its cool and plays with composure and sportsmanship will not only enjoy the game more but be more successful. The players will also observe the impact coaches and officials, presumably adults, have on the behavior of the players. Hopefully, their effect will be a positive one.

b) Statistics Charts

Players may be asked to attend a game and keep a close record of shots taken, shots missed, rebounds, turnovers, assists, etc.

   Learning Outcomes

   These statistics combined with their own subjective observations should allow players to reach their own conclusions about the level of play of that game.

c) Scouting Reports

Players might be asked to take notes on the play of a particular team, recording both individual and team characteristics.

   Learning Outcomes

   Players will develop a more intelligent approach to the game and begin to see themselves as students of the game of basketball rather than fans.

d) Coaching Interview

Players might be asked to interview a coach after a game using a prepared list of questions. Responses may be either recorded or noted and subsequently transcribed.

   Learning Outcomes

   Players will begin to understand the reasons the game took the direction it did. Players will develop a more critical attitude towards the strategies employed.

e) A Photo Essay

Players might be asked to prepare a pictorial essay of a particular aspect of the game of basketball. It would be urged at this point not to make a collection of random photographs but rather to collect the photographs that are of a similar theme, rebounding, shooting, dribbling, etc.

Learning Outcomes

The facts players have learned in the lessons about the various fundamentals should be reinforced by a close examination of the pictures. Players should also be encouraged to criticize improper skill execution if it appears in the pictures.

f) Game Report

Players may be asked to write and submit a game report to a local newspaper. Some preparation is necessary in finding out the sort of things that a newspaper might deem newsworthy. It may be worthwhile to call a reporter who normally covers high school sport activities.

Learning Outcomes

Players will develop their writing skills and secondly, they will be forced to draw specific conclusions from the game they have just observed.

g) Two-on-Two Tournament

Players should organize a two-on-two tournament for a school that could be run at lunch time and administered totally from the players in the basketball class.

Learning Outcomes

Players develop their organizational skills. Players practice their officiating.

h) Rule Changes

Players may be asked to make three proposals for rule changes or additions. A case should be prepared in anticipation of any opposition. This is a very difficult assignment and may require some questioning of officials and coaches.

Learning Outcomes

Players become aware of the philosophy behind the rules. Players become aware of the differences between the International Amateur Basketball Federation (FIBA) and National Collegiate Athletic Association (NCAA) rules.

i) Statistics Sheet

Players may be asked to design a better statistic sheet. In order to do so they should canvas the various basketball teams in the area for copies of their statistics sheets. Ideally, this newly developed sheet should allow one person to record everything that takes place during the game.

Learning Outcomes

Players become aware of all aspects of the game of basketball from scoring to rebounds to ball control.

3. Affective

While a variety of affective assessment techniques could be employed, subjective evaluation by the instructor should consider attitude, active participation, cooperation, sportsmanship and leadership.

Appendix I
Reference Material

A. Books

Bain, Robert; Hayes, Doug; Quance, Al. *Level II Technical Coaching Manual.* Ottawa, Basketball Canada, 1980.

Brace, David K. *Basketball Skills Test for Girls.* Aapher Publications. Washington, D.C., 1966.

Brace, David K. *Basketball Skills Test for Boys.* Aapher Publications. Washington, D.C., 1966.

Cousy, Bob and Power, Frank G. Jr. *Basketball Concepts and Techniques.* Boston: Allyn and Bacon, Inc., 1970.

Mitchelson, Barry. *Level I Technical Coaching Manual.* Ottawa, Basketball Canada, 1978.

Newell, Pete and Benington, John. *Basketball Methods.* New York: The Ronald Press Company, 1962.

Rush, Cathy. *Women's Basketball.* New York, Hawthorne Books Inc. 1976.

Turnbull, Anne C. *Basketball For Women.* Don Mills, Ontario, Addison-Wesley Publishing Company, 1973.

Wooden, John R. *Practical Modern Basketball.* New York: The Ronald Press Company, 1966.

Wooden, John R. and Sharman, Bill. *The Wooden-Sharman Method: A Guide to Winning Basketball.* New York: Macmillan Publishing Co. Inc., 1975.

B. Audio Visual Resources

Films and video resources for loan or purchase are available at:

B.C. Film Library
800 Hornby Street
Vancouver B.C.

Coaches Association of Canada
333 River Road
Vanier, Ontario
K1L 8B9

C. Basketball Associations

The national governing body for Basketball is:

Basketball Canada
333 River Road
Vanier, Ontario
K1L 8B9

The one organization that relates to all Basketball played in British Columbia is the B.C. Amateur Basketball Association. The National Coaching Certification Program, the purpose of which is to upgrade the level of coaching in Canada, is administered by the BCABA.

For information regarding the dates and location of coaching clinics, as well as details on any aspect of the game, please contact:

B.C. Amateur Basketball Association
1200 Hornby Street
Vancouver B.C. V6Z 2E2
Phone: 687-3333

Affiliated organizations which may be contacted through the BCABA are:

BC Basketball Officials Association
BC Association of Basketball Coaches
BC High School Boys' Basketball Association
BC Secondary School Girls' Basketball Association

Appendix II
Dr. James Naismith's Original Basketball Rules

The first basketball game was played in December 1891 according to the following 13 rules:

1. The ball may be thrown in any direction with one or both hands.
2. The ball may be batted in any direction with one or both hands (never with the fist).
3. A player cannot run with the ball. The player must throw it from the spot on which he catches it, allowance to be made for a man who catches the ball when running if he tries to stop.
4. The ball must be held in or between the hands, the arms or body must not be used for holding it.
5. No shouldering, holding, pushing, tripping, or striking in any way the person of an opponent shall be allowed; the first infringement of this rule by any person shall count as foul, the second shall disqualify him until the next goal is made, or, if there was evident intent to injure the person, for the whole of the game, no substitute allowed.
6. A foul is striking at the ball with the fist, violations of Rules 3, 4 and such as described in Rule 5.
7. If either side makes three consecutive fouls, it shall count as a goal for the opponents (consecutive means without the opponent in the mean time making a foul).
8. A goal shall be made when the ball is thrown or batted from the grounds into the basket and stays there, providing those defending the goal do not touch or disturb the goal.
9. When the ball goes out of bounds, it shall be thrown into the field and played by the person first touching it. He has a right to hold it unmolested for five seconds. In case of a dispute the umpire shall throw it straight into the field. The thrower-in is allowed five seconds, if he holds it longer it shall go to the opponent. If any side persists in delaying the game the umpire shall call a foul on that side.
10. The umpire shall be the judge of the men and shall note the fouls and notify the referee when three consecutive fouls have been made. He shall have the power to disqualify men according to Rule 5.
11. The referee shall be the judge of the ball and shall decide when the ball is in play, in bounds, to which side it belongs, and shall keep the time. He shall decide when a goal has been made, and keep account of the goals, with any other duties that are usually performed by a referee.
12. The time shall be two fifteen minutes' halves, with five minutes rest between.
13. The side making the most goals in that time shall be declared the winners. In case of a draw the game may, by agreement of the captains, be continued until another goal is made.

Dr. James Naismith, the game's inventor, was born in Almonte, Ontario in 1861. At the request of the head of the physical training department of the Springfield, Massachusetts Y.M.C.A., Naismith was asked to create an indoor game to fill the winter season void between football and baseball.

With remarkable swiftness, the news of this new game spread throughout North America.

Appendix III
Glossary

Arc: The path of the ball towards the basket on a shot.

Backboard: The vertical plane to which the basket is attached.

Back court: The other half of the court in which team A defends the basket.
*Note: Team A's back court would be Team B's front court and vice versa.

Ball cut: A player without the ball moves quickly towards the ball in an attempt to get free from his defensive counterpart to receive the ball.

Ball handling: The skill of controlling the ball in all situations.

Ball side: The side of the front court where the ball is.

Baseline: The boundaries of the basketball court at either end.

Basic athletic position: Knees flexed, back straight. Feet slightly wider than shoulder width. Chin over the toes.

Block: An offensive maneuver in which a player offers himself as a stationary obstacle which a team mate may use to shake free from the player guarding him.

Block out: The ability to prevent an opponent from recovering a rebound by stepping between the opponent and the ball.

Dribble: A method of moving the ball by bouncing it while running.

Fast break: A style of play in which a rebound is recovered by the defensive team and moved quickly down the court for an attempted field goal.

Field goal: Any shot taken from the playing area while the clock is running. Value two points.

Forward: An offensive and defensive position played between the foul line extended and the baseline

Foul: An infraction of the rules usually in the area of excessive contact.

Foul shot or free throw: A shot resulting from a penalty which gives a player an unobstructed shot from the free throw line. Value one point.

Front court: The half of the playing surface in which team A attempts to score.

Full court press: A defensive tactic in which the defense contests the ball and the opponents in every part of the playing area.

Fundamentals: The basic skills of passing, shooting and ball handling necessary to play the game effectively.

Give and go: An effective play in which one member of the offensive team passes the ball to a teammate and cuts towards the basket in anticipation of a return pass.

Guard: An offensive and defensive position normally played between the free throw line extended and the half court line.

Jump ball: A contest in which the ball is tossed between two players to a point higher than either can jump. The players attempt to tip the ball to team mates waiting outside the jump circle.

Jump shot: A shot taken during a jump in an attempt to release the ball from a point higher than the defensive player can reach.

Key:	The restricted area bounded by the free throw line, baseline and the two lines which connect them. An offensive player may remain in the key or restricted area for only three seconds (see page 7).
Lay up shot:	A short shot taken very close to the basket generally after a dribble or pass.
Man to man defense:	Style of play in which each defensive player has been assigned the task of preventing one player on the offence from scoring.
Mid court line:	This line divides the playing area in half.
Pivot:	An offensive movement in which the player who has the ball keeps one foot anchored in position and moves the other foot so as to create a better passing angle or to protect the ball from an opponent.
Post or center:	The post player stands on or near the perimeter of the restricted area or key with back to the basket. Normally a team's tallest player.
Rebound:	A missed field goal attempt.
Scrimmage:	A part of a basketball practice that most resembles game conditions. Generally teams are always comprised of five players and all the rules of the game are observed.
Set shot:	A shot taken from a stationary position.
Three point play:	A player who scores a field goal, is fouled while shooting and is given a free throw which, if made, will result in a total of three points being scored.
Three-to-make-two:	A player fouled in the act of shooting whose field goal attempt is unsuccessful is given three opportunities to score two free throws. This play is unique to F.I.B.A. or international rules.
Time out:	Any period during which play is stopped.
Weak side:	The half of the front court where the ball is not.
Zone defense:	A style of play in which all defensive players adjust their movements to movements of the goal.

Sports Handbook Series

Tennis Handbook
Graphics illustrate grips and strokes in this compact guide to a popular sport. Everything necessary to teach - and play - is tucked between the covers.
ISBN 0-88839-049-1

Folk Dance Handbook
The fascinating complexities of this activity are set out in a clear, easy-to-follow format that should bring the delights of folk dance within the reach of everyone.
ISBN 0-88839-044-0

Soccer Handbook
Skills and how to teach them; drills and when to use them; plus detailed plans for sequential teaching of the game. Compact yet comprehensive.
ISBN 0-88839-048-3

Field Hockey Handbook
Concise, clearly illustrated, a useful guide to learning and teaching a fast-growing sport.
ISBN 0-88839-043-2

Basketball Handbook
Rules and activities are clearly illustrated to make this guide indispensable to anyone coaching or teaching the game.
ISBN 0-88839-042-4

Badminton Handbook
A well-illustrated guide to all the basics of the game, this also includes a discussion of teaching strategies when player skills vary widely.
ISBN 0-88839-041-6

Men's Gymnastics Handbook
Teaching sequences for the six Olympic events of men's artistic gymnastics are explained in detail, with precise information on spotting and safety techniques providing valuable guidance for the instructor.
ISBN 0-88839-046-7

Women's Gymnastics Handbook
A detailed guide to the teaching of gymnastic skills for women, including lesson plans and methods for evaluating performers.
ISBN 0-88839-045-9

Orienteering Handbook
The rapidly-growing interest in this activity makes the publication of this book particularly timely. It includes detailed information on basic concepts, setting a course and organizing a meet, as well as addresses for obtaining equipment and other resources.
ISBN 0-88839-047-5

ALSO AVAILABLE

Safety in Gymnastics *by Gerald A. Carr Phd.* A comprehensive guide to spotting and safety techniques in the gymnasium. 600 sequential illustrations. ISBN 0-99939-054-8 $12.95

Curling Handbook *by Roy D. Theissen.* The history of the game, complete, detailed. ISBN 0-919654-71-1 $5.95

Tennis: The Decision-Making Sport *by Josef Brabenec.* Think your way to victory on the court with Canada's national tennis coach. ISBN 0-88839-052-1 $9.95